I have enormous respect

for the comic strip as a

potential story and art

form, although far too few

of its productions have

realized that potential.

If those few, however,

could be gathered into some

sort of complete collection,

the effect on those who

have scorned the comics as

a whole might well be

devastating. . . .

Edmund Wilson
from a letter to Bill Blackbeard
1966

The **Smithsonian** Collection of NEWSPAPER COMICS

Edited by **Bill Blackbeard** and **Martin Williams**

Foreword by **John Canaday**

Copublished by Smithsonian Institution Press

and **Harry N. Abrams, Inc.**

Note to reader   **The comic strips in this book are numbered in the order in which they are reproduced. References in the text and index to particular strips are indicated by those
numbers in brackets.**

Frontispiece: *Johnny Wise*, 1902, by Tad Dorgan.

Library of Congress Cataloging in Publication Data
Smithsonian Institution.
   The Smithsonian collection of newspaper comics.
   Bibliography: p.
   Includes index.
   1.   Comic books, strips, etc.—United States.
I.   Blackbeard, Bill.   II.   Williams, Martin T.
III.   Title.
PN6726.S5   1977   741.5′973   77-608090
Smithsonian Institution Press, Washington, D.C. 20560
ISBN 0-87474-172-6   ISBN 0-87474-167-X pbk
Harry N. Abrams, Inc., New York 10022
ISBN 8109-1612-6   ISBN 8109-2081-6 pbk

Designed by Elizabeth Sur
Printed and bound in Japan. All rights reserved.
Third printing

The cartoons referred to here by strip numbers are reprinted with the permission of:

Chicago Tribune-New York News Syndicate: 23, 96-107, 128-129, 138-139, 151-156, 221-277, 438-441, 644-715, 720-722, 740, 760
Robert C. Dille: 427-428
Edgar Rice Burroughs, Inc.: 429
Field Newspaper Syndicate: 3-4, 11-14, 20, 22, 126-127, 142, 505-539, 755-757, 759
Johnny Hart: 755, 757
I.H.T. Corporation: 126-127, 142
Crockett Johnson: 505-539
Jack Kent: 744-749
Selby Kelly: 734-737
King Features: 5-10, 32-37, 40, 47-83, 92-95, 130-135, 140-141, 144-150, 157-161, 170-174, 278-319, 430-431, 444-484, 718, 723-733, 750-753, 758, 761-763
Mell Lazarus: 756, 759
McNaught Syndicate, Inc.: 28-29, 41-46, 108-125, 136-137, 163-169, 540-541
Newspaper Enterprise Association: 175-178, 320-426, 432-437, 497-504
The Philadelphia Inquirer: 162
Scripps-Howard Newspapers: 1, 15, 19, 24-27, 30-31, 38-39, 716-717
The Seattle Times: 84-91
Skippy, Inc.: 174
Jessie Kahles Straut: 143
Warren Tufts: 741
United Features Syndicate: 738-739, 742-743
Universal Press Syndicate: 754
Raeburn Van Buren: 485-496
Walt Disney Productions: 542-643

Contents

Foreword

You have to be lucky enough to have been around for a rather long stretch of years—say seven decades—to remember a time when newspaper comics were just newspaper comics rather than sociological documents and works of art with their own set of innovative esthetic principles, which they have become. If you have been really lucky, luckier than all but a handful of people I know, the comics are tied to the time when you were a small boy in a small town about a hundred miles from Kansas City and your weekly reward for good behavior in Sunday school was five cents for a copy of the Sunday *Kansas City Star*. Along with reports of the sinking of the Titanic in 1912, the declaration of war in Europe in 1914, and other events in the fictional area outside a ten-mile radius from the Bourbon County Court House in Fort Scott, the *Star* kept you abreast of the adventures of the Katzenjammer Kids, Happy Hooligan, Buster Brown, and other familiar personalities of the real world.

The transmutation of the old newspaper comics from their initial character as entertainments to be read lying on your stomach on the floor before Sunday dinner, into their current status as sociological testaments for intellectual evaluation, as demonstrated by this book, pleases me, since it is always reassuring to see that solid respectability may follow thoughtless youth. But my own response to the comics reproduced here is not at all intellectual. The early ones reduce me to a quivering jelly of nostalgia, which is the condition of remembering how sweet life used to be and forgetting how terrible it was. This holds up to about the time I was eight, when we moved from Kansas to Texas.

The years from eight to twelve were my collector's period, with suit boxes filled with thousands of strips clipped from daily papers and filed by date and subject. Upon entering high school I threw the collection out as kid stuff, and for the next four years the comics, although assiduously followed, occupied a residual spot in my attention, badgered as I was, as everybody is at that time, by geysers of hormones. The trouble with having been lucky enough to know newspaper comics shortly after 1907 and up to 1919 is that you have to settle for the 1920s for your teen-age years, and there never was a much more embarrassing time for an adult to look back on. Teenagers since then have passed through more dangerous, more violent, and more tragic periods, but not more embarrassing ones. We were silly, let's let it go at that.

The point in mentioning that period here is that in spite of so much that is painful to recall, my early 'teens were marked by one discovery that saves my self-respect. This was *Krazy Kat*. Krazy was not a general favorite with my contemporaries—adolescent or adult. They liked Barney Google and Moon Mullins. So did I. The more sophisticated of my colleagues went for *Toonerville Trolley*. So did I. But they couldn't see what was funny about *Krazy Kat*, nor could they see that that was exactly the point—that Krazy *wasn't* funny. He/she was (is, and surely always will be) a combination of a lot of things, including hilarious, but not funny.

In 1926 Gilbert Seldes in *The Seven Lively Arts* wrote the famous essay on Krazy, celebrating Kokonino Kounty and its inhabitants on a philosophical premise identifying Krazy with Don Quixote, but this was several years after I used to go through the Strouds's discarded copies of the *San Antonio Light* to find Krazy. My father refused to have a Hearst paper in the house and the Strouds, less fussy, lived next door.

Whenever self-doubts as to my intellectual capacity, my poetic sensitivity, my critical acumen, or my humanistic discernment threaten to sink me, I can always surface on my record as a precocious member of what was to become a Kult. Krazy also saved me later in life: The only explanation I can see as to why my mistakes as a parent didn't scar my offspring is that Krazy, by then collected in a book with another appreciation by e e cummings, was always at hand instead of the literary pap usually fed to kiddies. Within the family we mastered Krazy's dialect for use on special occasions, and could recite back and forth the dialogues from favorite episodes. It sounds precious and would have been precious if there had been anything self-conscious or Kultish about it, but it wasn't like that. Krazy was a kind of pet, mascot, and Keeper of the Peace around our house, a benign presence and good example even today from his/her spot on the bookshelf.

Somehow I never managed to get really involved with any of the comics later than Krazy—a loss for me, I'm sure, which this book may correct. There was a brief period at the University of Virginia when it was voguish among the young professors to pretend to be fascinated with Mary Worth. We would tell each other we could hardly wait to find out how she would straighten out so-and-so's troubles. But it was all pretty phony, a kind of reverse academicism. During those years I remember also stumbling over stacks of comic books upstairs in the boys' room, probably Buck Rogers and Superman operating on different wave lengths from Krazy's in the library downstairs. But I never looked into these.

So I lost track of the comics. The closest I ever came to post-Krazy involvement was in the spring of 1944, serving in the Marine Corps with Alex Raymond, who relinquished the authorship of *Flash Gordon* in order to enlist with a group of officer-trainees at Quantico, Virginia. Raymond was held in downright veneration by the rest of the class; even the drill sergeant, who was otherwise the meanest man in the world, regarded him as a rare and fragile object that might shatter if commanded to shoulder arms in too rough a tone of voice, giving me some idea of the power that comics still held in America—and, I am sure, still do.

The comics are ubiquitous. You don't have to have followed a strip for its identity to have somehow entered your consciousness: the comics affect your way of feeling about the daily world whether or not you read them. So far as I can tell, the effect on me has been salutary, and I am content with the idea of strengthening it with the aid of this anthology. The function of art, we are told, is to clarify, intensify, or enlarge our experience, and the comics are now art. Without much expectation of clarification, or of intensification, let me now set about expanding my boundaries. In the meanwhile, although grateful for this book, I am also grateful for the time-scheme that allowed me to know the comics when.

John Canaday
New York, May 17, 1977

Acknowledgments

The names of the many syndicates and individual artists who have generously contributed to this volume appear on the comics pages which follow. Here we would like especially to thank the following:

King Features Syndicate and Charlotte MacCleary

Field Newspaper Syndicate

Mell Lazarus

The late Crockett Johnson

Selby Kelly

Robert S. Reed and the Chicago Tribune-New York News Syndicate

Johnny Hart

David Stolberg and the Scripps-Howard Newspapers

Charles V. McAdam and the McNaught Syndicate

Robert C. Dille

Jessie Kahles Straut

Thomas E. Peoples and the Newspaper Enterprise Association

Joan Crosby Tibbets

Raeburn Van Buren

Edgar Rice Burroughs, Inc., and Robert M. Hodes

The I. H. T. Corporation

Jack Kent and Stanleigh Arnold

William Ravenscroft and United Features Syndicate

Walt Disney Productions

Universal Press Syndicate

and, finally, Rick Marschall

Sports writers . . . are surpassed in ingenuity and success as diligent coiners of neologisms only by the comic strip artists, of whom Thomas A. (Tad) Dorgan, Elzie Crisler Segar and Billy De Beck are examples. Dorgan . . . is said to have invented or introduced drugstore cowboy, nobody home . . . and to have launched such popular phrases as 'You tell him,' 'Yes, we have no bananas,' and 'You said it.' Segar (creator of Popeye) is credited with goon, jeep, and various other terms that, in the hands of others, took on wide extensions of meaning, and with starting the vogue for the words ending in burger. To De Beck . . . are ascribed heebie jeebies, hot mamma, hotsy-totsy, and horse feathers. . . . The comic strip artist . . . has been a very diligent maker of terse and dramatic words. In his grim comments upon the horrible calamities which befall his characters he not only employs many ancients of English speech, e.g., slam, bang, quack, mee-ow, smash and bump, but also invents novelties of his own, e.g., zowie, bam, socko, yurp, plop, wow, wham, glug, oof, ulk, whap, bing, fooie and grrr. . . . Their influence upon the general American vocabulary must be very potent. . . .

H. L. Mencken
The American Language, 1919, and Supplement One, 1945

Introduction

The Comic Treasures of the

American Newspaper Page

I

The elements of the American comic strip were already there. A succession of drawings expressing a continuous action, an anecdotal event, a narrative—they are as old as cave paintings and had been vividly rendered in European art, in Greek temple reliefs, and in Giotto frescoes. "Talk balloons," speeches offered in encircled, smoke-like wisps from the mouths of characters, were fairly common in eighteenth-century caricature, and graphic caricature was fairly commonplace by the mid-nineteenth century. And so, in the British "comic papers," were captioned cartoon narratives offering, usually in broad burlesque, farcical incident and anecdote which largely derived from the conventions of circus clowning and the music hall-vaudeville sketch.

It remained for the United States, then entering fully into its own era of mass communications, to put all these elements together and make something new of them, something new and compelling, and so irresistible that it spread (along with our movies and our music) around the world.

Only in the past decade has the American newspaper comic strip begun to be recognized in its own country as an innovative and creative cultural accomplishment. It has long been hailed in France and elsewhere in Europe as one of the important achievements in the arts of this century, and it has been studiously examined there in a number of journals exclusively devoted to the subject.

That is perhaps not so exceptional or extreme a cultural default as it may at first seem. Notoriously, Europeans—and particularly the French—have recognized, researched, praised (and sometimes overpraised) the American arts—our movies, our jazz, our comics—before we have. And it would perhaps not be too chauvinistic to point out that we have produced those things, after all, and loved them, and that scholarship, art criticism, and cultural history are secondary pursuits.

At the same time, many of our own historians of the arts, having borrowed their principles, procedures, and attitudes largely from European cultural historians, have proceeded to apply those principles only to such traditional categories as we have borrowed directly from abroad—to literary history, to the theater, to concert music, and the like, sometimes pausing to scorn or reject those artistic genres that are particularly American, like the movies, jazz, and the comics. Europeans, meanwhile, have applied their principles of cultural history and criticism in modified form to those American creations and transmutations which we still think of as our "popular" or even our "light" artistic pursuits.

Thus the comic strip has been critically neglected in the United States, and has even been openly attacked. But a further, and perhaps crucial reason for the neglect of the comics lay in the aversion of most well-educated Americans of every political persuasion for the sensational press of the turn of the century and later. The professors, teachers, prelates, and literati of the time usually did not see these newspapers as colorful and amusing but saw them instead as vicious, crude, and frightening in their instant and openly demagogic appeal to a mass readership. And the papers they most grimly eschewed—the Hearst titles connected in a chain from coast to coast, the *Chicago Tribune*, the *New York World* (until 1920), the *New York Daily News* —were precisely the papers which carried the largest array of comic strips by the most talented artists. The papers most respected and read by these educators and tastemakers—the *New York Times*, the *New York Herald Tribune*, the *Boston Transcript*, the *Baltimore Sun*—carried fewer strips, and the *Times* carried (and carries) none at all.

Comics seemed to the elite the obviously lowbrow Pied Piper which lured the innocents to their journalistic doom at the hands of the Hearsts, McCormicks, and Pulitzers. Weren't *Krazy Kat, Little Nemo, Buster Brown, Happy Hooligan,* and the *Katzenjammer Kids* being paid for and distributed by Hearst? They must therefore be tainted by his political ambitions and social attitudes; any intrinsic merit they might possess as works of art was perhaps accidental, certainly irrelevant, and surely best ignored.

The majority of those in authoritative positions in American literature and art during the first half of this century simply may not have seen the more subtly imaginative, gorgeously inventive, and creatively memorable strips at all because these exciting works were being published in the wrong papers. And concomitantly, they overlooked the colorfully bound strip reprint volumes issued by minor publishers at the time, both as entertainment for themselves and as gifts for their children.

At the same time, even the most gifted and creatively involved comic-strip artists tended to hold themselves and their work in a modest and unpretentious low regard. They made small jokes about their strips in public, surrendered their original art to their employing syndicates without expecting or wanting its return, supplied funny anecdotes for superficial articles about their careers, sighed after "serious" art pursuits, and—perhaps worst for the historian— maintained virtually no reference files of their own work.

Similarly, our libraries have been negligent. Many would not even stock the *New York Graphic* or certain of the Hearst newspapers. Only one substantial book has ever been devoted to the *Graphic,* possibly the most iconoclastically innovative newspaper in American history. A scant half dozen have been written about Hearst's highly important chain of journals. And none has yet appeared on the *New York Daily News* or the *Chicago Tribune.* A side result was the failure of the New York Public Library to maintain any comprehensive file of Hearst's *New York Journal,* crucial to the study of journalism as well as to that of the comic strip. And indeed the *New York Graphic* has apparently not survived at all; there may be no file of that paper, public or private, left on earth.

Had the comic-strip material which ran in the shunned popular press been published instead by *Vanity Fair* or *The New Yorker,* or had it reached the august pages of the *New York Times,* there can be little doubt that the best examples of the strip form would have readily received the critical accolades and appreciative discussion they should have had from the outset. As it is, we have missed such theoretical rewards as H. L. Mencken's comments on E. C. Segar's *Thimble Theatre* as Americana and sustained comic narrative; Lionel Trilling's consideration of the renovation of the Dickensian character in the literature of the comic strip; Kenneth Burke's analysis of linguistic symbol and graphic leitmotif in the popular mythos of the strips; and Edmund Wilson's consideration of the potential of Edward Gorey's working with the sustained characters and narrative of the comic strip.

Still and all, there have been some nine studies of historical and critical substance dealing with the newspaper strips published in the United States since 1897. Perhaps there is some record of appreciation of a national art form after all.

II

This collection presents, in a single volume, an extensive gallery of newspaper comics, an anthology which the editors hope offers some memorable and amusing art and narrative.

The comic strip is essentially a narrative art. A well-conceived story, character, or incident can make clumsy or barely competent art work functionally acceptable, much as a strong story and good character actors may redeem films with slipshod camera and directorial work. Indeed, some strip artists were, by strict standards of draftsmanship or graphics, no artists at all. What they had was a point of view (a sometimes rowdy point of view, to be sure) on the human animal and his attitudes and actions, and a functional means to convey it.

Still, the art of the comic strip did provide an extraordinary vehicle for inspired graphic experimentation and accomplishment by some major comic-strip artists, including Winsor McCay, Lyonel Feininger, George Herriman, Cliff Sterrett, Roy Crane, Milton Caniff, and others whom the reader will readily note in the following pages.

As we indicate, however, it was as a challenge to the storytelling imagination that the comic strip stirred its most striking response among creative minds, and it brought to light a number of talents who were able to use its highly individual techniques of continuity to often remarkable advantage. Compare, for example, the graphic competence of Roy Crane in his *Wash Tubbs* story in this volume with that of E. C. Segar in the *Thimble Theatre* narrative. Crane's sensitive mastery of pictorial composition and technique is self-evident (his panels in the *Tubbs* whaling sequences are as deftly evocative of the cetacean majesty and movement as Rockwell Kent's illustrations for *Moby Dick*), and they are in sharp contrast to Segar's obviously limited graphic concerns. However, both artist-narrators were readily able to spin stories of arresting incident, humor, strong characterizations, and sustained plot interest, and few readers can resist the compulsion to read their narratives raptly through to the end.

Thus the dual purpose of this collection reflects the remarkable dichotomy of the strip medium itself, shared only with cinema, in that its best works can be enjoyed both as "gallery" art and in continuity as fiction or drama.

Indeed, this division of esthetic possibility is reflected in the divergent emphases of the only two national institutions at present devoted in full or great part to comic-strip art: the Museum of Cartoon Art in Greenwich, Connecticut, which is largely concerned with rotating displays of original strip drawings; and the San Francisco Academy of Comic Art, which files all of the printed strips, so they can be studied in relation to other printed narrative arts, as story-carrying material.

III

The comic strip may functionally be defined as a serially published, episodic, open-ended dramatic narrative or series of linked anecdotes about recurrent, identified characters, told in successive drawings regularly enclosing ballooned dialogue or its equivalent and minimized narrative text.

Not all the features contained herein fit that functional definition, in detail, to be sure. Johnny Gruelle's *Mr. Twee Deedle*, for example, has no ballooned dialogue and might actually be considered a kind of comic version of an illustrated children's book. Similarly, the comics page *Tarzan*, in any of its several versions over the years, is a condensed-narrative, fantasy-adventure tale in text-and-illustration form.

The American comic strip first attained definitive form in a Sunday *Yellow Kid* page, drawn by Richard Felton Outcault for William Randolph Hearst's *American Humorist* weekly comic supplement to his *New York Journal*, on October 18, 1896.

The immediate progenitor of the comic strip was probably the illustrated novel of the nineteenth century, which in England, France, and the United States usually featured caricature and cartoon art as intimate accompaniment to the texts of such popular authors as Dickens, Thackeray, Balzac, Hugo, and others. But the strip failed to

develop as an immediate outgrowth of the reading public's enormous relish for cartoon-supported narrative in the 1830s and 1840s. A Pickwick comic strip, issued in bound parts by the same publisher who originally hired Dickens to write text for the popular cartoons of Robert Seymour, thus bringing *Pickwick Papers* into being, might seem in retrospect to have been a likely event. With art by Phiz (Hablot Knight Browne) and script and balloon dialogue by Dickens, such a work might well have had wide popularity. But it would have taken a prescient imagination to conceive of a full-fledged fictional narrative being carried forward by means of dialogue within successive drawings, much as drama was performed on a stage, and without need of extensive prose explication. Such an imagination did not exist in Dickens's time, not even in his own fertile and graphically oriented mind.

Any narrative that was presented by means of short sets of successive drawings was largely limited to pantomimic pratfall gags and occasional simplistic political parables. In these forms, captions and dialogue, whether presented outside or within the panels, essentially served as embellishment to the art. In the Outcault *Yellow Kid* of October 18, 1896, however, the whole point of the vaudeville gag depended on the dialogue between the Kid and the parrot, and that was the first time this had occurred in a graphic work which also met the other prerequisites of the strip form.

Both Outcault's publisher, Hearst, and his fellow cartoonists on the staff of the *American Humorist* were quick to perceive and to pursue the broad possibilities the Yellow Kid's turn with a comic-dialogue payoff had for the comic-character features the *Humorist* was then emphasizing. The crucial and relevant effect of rapidly exchanged dialogue in a Weber and Fields vaudeville skit could now be paralleled in comic art. Possibly Outcault's innovation struck the *Humorist* staff in something of the same way that the direct addition of sound to film struck most workers in the silent-movie industry, startling them into a realization of expressive possibilities undreamed of. Cartoonists of the time had long been wedded to the notion that art of any kind should exist well apart from prose exposition, like a kind of frozen tableau.

Outcault himself promptly seized with relish on the potential of the art form he had created, enlarging on the dialogue and prose essentials of the comic strip with pioneering gusto and imagination, as did his companions in the new field. By the turn of the century, dialogue and art had been commonly wedded in the newspaper comics. And by the 1930s comics in which dialogue was minimal or nonexistent, such as J. Carver Pusey's *Benny* and Carl Anderson's *Henry*, were regarded as inventive and original in their refreshing departure from convention.

Prolonged graphic narrative was an obvious step for cartoonists turning out weekly newspaper strips to take, and two of Outcault's confreres on the Hearst *Journal*, Rudolph Dirks (whose *Katzenjammer Kids* had entertained readers since 1896) and Fred Opper (the creator of the comic strip's own divine and Dostoevskian Idiot, *Happy Hooligan*) were the first to carry thematic concepts from one week's strip episode to the next. Other early strip artists to enlarge on narrative possibilities and to develop actual cliff-hanging suspense were Lyonel Feininger in his *Kin-der-Kids* for the *Chicago Tribune* in 1906, Winsor McCay in *Little Nemo in Slumberland* for the *New York Herald* in 1905, and Charles W. Kahles in *Hairbreadth Harry* for the *Philadelphia Press* in 1906.

Weekday comic strips in black and white were initiated in the Hearst morning and afternoon papers across the country in the early 1900s. At first, these were miniaturized versions of the Sunday comic strips, self-contained gags about reappearing characters for whom the strips were named. (Some early examples were Gus Mager's *Knocko the Monk*, H. A. McGill's *Padlock Bones, the Dead Sure Detective,* and F. M. Howarth's *Mr. E. Z. Mark.*) Some might appear for as many as ten successive weekdays, but that was accidental; the average frequency was three days a week, and the editorial purpose was to provide daily variety in strips, not daily duplication of the same features.

In 1907, however, Henry Conway "Bud" Fisher, sports-page cartoonist for the *San Francisco Chronicle,* introduced a seven-day-a-week sports-page comic strip called *A. Mutt,* which gave the reader daily, tongue-in-cheek horse-racing tips. Mr. Mutt suffered or prospered according to the next-day outcome of these tips.

Fisher had, in fact, gotten his idea for the *Chronicle* feature from an earlier but ill-fated try for a similar strip created by Clare Briggs and Moses Koenigsberg for the Hearst Chicago papers, the *American* and *Examiner.* Called *A. Piker Clerk,* the Briggs-drawn sports-page strip, primarily an *American* feature, was intended for daily publication, but was late for many of the paper's several daily editions and was crowded out of others by late sports news. Finally given the coup de disgrace by Hearst—who found Briggs's twitting of foreign dignitaries (i.e., the Czar of Russia) in the strip vulgar—*A. Piker Clerk* remains a vital if premature experiment in developing a daily comic strip.

Fisher's *A. Mutt* (later *Mutt and Jeff*) literally became an overnight sensation in San Francisco and materially increased the daily circulation of the *Chronicle.* The paper's bitter local rival, the Hearst *Examiner,* sensed a good thing in the strip and promptly hired Fisher away from the *Chronicle* at a hefty boost in salary. The local delight with Fisher's daily episode continued, and the impressed Hearst wasted no time in moving Fisher to New York and syndicating *A. Mutt* nationally. An aroused public's interest in daily character strips with strong thematic narrative was nurtured by a myriad of other six- and seven-day-a-week strips which quickly followed on the sports pages of papers everywhere, including Sidney Smith's *Buck Nix* in the *Chicago American,* Russ Westover's *Luke McGluck* in the *San Francisco Post,* C. M. Payne's *Honeybunch's Hubby* in the *New York World,* and George Herriman's *Baron Mooch* in the *Los Angeles Examiner.*

On January 31, 1912, Hearst introduced the nation's first full daily comic page in his *New York Evening Journal,* adding it to his other afternoon papers from coast to coast a few days later. Initially made up of four large daily strips, including Herriman's *Family Upstairs* and Harry Hershfield's *Desperate Desmond* (a continuing cliff-hanger), the Hearst page expanded to five, then six, and finally nine daily strips through the teens and early twenties. Other papers emulated the Hearst example, and by the 1920s the phenomenon was to be found in hundreds of newspapers around the country, fed by dozens of daily strips distributed by a multitude of small syndicates. From these early small syndicates emerged the giants of the thirties, such as Hearst's King Features, Newspaper Enterprise Association (NEA), the Chicago Tribune–New York News Syndicate, the Associated Press, and United Features from United Press.

By the 1930s, comic strips by the daily pageful and Sunday color section collections were to be found in most American and Canadian newspapers. Vital to the then widespread urban and rural competition between newspapers, the comic strip was given increasing space and prominence, with editors vying for the newest, strongest, and most original. As a result, the comic strip was to be seen at its most varied, inventive, colorful, and exciting plenty in the thirties and early forties—a peak of creativity and popularity it has not held since.

IV

As an introductory collection, our volume has (and must have) its limitations. Eight strips are presented here in extensive continuity with complete narrative sequence, but perhaps as many as thirty deserve that kind of representation. Moreover, a number of fine strips have been crowded out of even the group of single-episode examples to which a large body of the included strips have been limited. But in order to establish a functional basis for the selection of representative material, the editors had to set a few general rules of procedure.

First, we drew up two lists of comics. One of them contained the editors' choices of the most accomplished and critically memorable strips, considered both as graphic and narrative works. The other set forth the most generally famed, popular, and typical strips. Thus *The Kin-der-Kids*, *Mr. Twee Deedle*, and *School Days* would be on the first list, but not the second; while *Tillie the Toiler* and *Joe Palooka* would be obvious choices for the second. A number of strips, of course, appeared on both lists (titles such as *Polly and Her Pals*, *Thimble Theatre*, *Katzenjammer Kids*, *Dick Tracy*, and *Mickey Mouse*), and clearly these were strong contenders for relatively extensive representation in the collection. The bulk of our volume is built around examples of those works which combine intrinsic excellence and wide popularity with readers of their time, while titles relegated to just one list or the other were included as space and the need for reasonable representation of both bodies of material seemed to dictate.

We also took into account those strips which have recently been so widely reprinted to meet the demands of their still-active aficionados that inclusion at length in these pages might be considered wasteful of valuable space—such strips as *Flash Gordon*, *Buck Rogers*, *Tarzan*, and *Prince Valiant*. *Dick Tracy* is included in a fairly long excerpt because of the nearly exclusive focus on the post-1940 strip in current reprints. Our selection is from the mid-thirties, when Chester Gould's work was rather different in quality and tone.

Ultimately, of course, what the editors have done in this collection is make their own choices out of their own knowledge and their own tastes. We may disagree as to whether every strip or every continuity herein is art or even artistic. We do not claim that the volume at hand is a "definitive" comics collection (whatever that would be). We have put together a selection of comics we feel are interesting, important, representative, funny, curious, exceptional, artistic—and the reader, of course, will take his choice from among those descriptions.

Further comments on the selections will be found in brief prefaces to each of the several period divisions of the book. Extensive discussion of all the material in this collection will be found in coeditor Bill Blackbeard's forthcoming book *The Endless Art: The Literature of the Comic Strip* (Oxford University Press).

On the matter of authorship, we make no effort to disentangle some knotty problems of strip history. A successful strip illustrator-author might hire an assistant to help draw, an assistant to help plot, or both, at one or more periods of his career—or, in some cases, an outright ghost or ghosts to take over for a while. Yet he still might retain an artistic control over his creation. (Or he might not. Indeed, the trade gossip has long held that the "author" of one of the most successful strips of the 1930s and 1940s never drew the feature at all, even in the beginning, and probably that gossip tells the truth. However, such matters are properly the province of other scholarship and other books.)

V

The pages that follow have their share of stereotypes and some of those stereotypes are racial. Comedy and melodrama are always based on the manipulation of stereotypes of some kind, although in such contexts we usually call them "stock characters" or "traditional types" or some such. What remains for the true artist, of course, is to bring his types to life and relate them to reality.

There is a distinction between a simply careless or insensitive or even racist exploitation of national and racial types on the one hand and a quite legitimate satire or burlesque on the other. But such distinctions are sometimes difficult to make, and American artists have not always made them.

The distinctions are important, to be sure. And you will find in these pages examples of both unthinking racial exploitation and, occasionally, true satirical observation. In the popular culture of this country, we are dealing with an art to which, until fairly recently, nothing and nobody was sacred. And in which a guileless Irish bum (*Happy Hooligan*), a confused black janitor, or a mysterious Oriental could be made the subject or the butt of humor or of melodrama, fairly or unfairly, without any hesitation.

At the same time, we are also sometimes the victims of our passing attitudes. Thus in the 1970s we are apt to find the conman Kingfish (although he was portrayed on television by a skillful black comedian, Tim Moore) disquieting. But we find Redd Foxx's Fred Sanford of "Sanford and Son" comfortably amusing. And we acclaim Richard Pryor's satiric array of scatological black street characters as examples of bold and insightful theatrical art.

Collective attitudes change. Perhaps popular insight changes as well. But comedy and drama both remain, and so, therefore, do the basic types that are a part of their substance.

In any case, as presented here they are a part of our history, a part which it would be pointless for us to attempt to suppress.

The question of content and meaning in these strips is one we do not intend to pursue further in this introduction. But it is a question quite worth pursuing, and one that would encompass collective and archetypical ritual; theatrical, literary, and graphic tradition; and contemporary social attitudes, conscious and unconscious.

It would involve the individual strip author's intentions as well. Harold Gray's *Little Orphan Annie* clearly invites us to admire the sizable empire-and-fortune-building prowess of Daddy Warbucks on the one hand, and the thrifty and loyal virtues the author sees as encouraged by day-to-day poverty on the other. Similarly, *Dick Tracy* was frankly conceived by Chester Gould as a policeman who would save us from rampant 1930s gangsterism by shooting first and asking questions afterwards.

VI

As indicated, much of the text of this volume represents the collaborative effort of both editors. As a result, the stylistic habits of each writer have been set aside to produce a harmoniously unobtrusive body of information to accompany the much more important graphic content of the book. Such opinions and historical interpretations as are set forth indicate only that one or the other of us held them; not necessarily both.

The current material in Section Eight, included to augment the general appeal of the collection and necessarily limited in scope through space considerations, was chosen mainly for its stylistic or thematic relation to the older and earlier material in the book and does not represent, by any means, all of the current titles either or both of us would like to have included.

By collecting and juxtaposing our strips as we have here, we do them some admitted injustice. The narratives of Segar, Kelly, and the rest are, after all, intended to be read in daily episodes, and each such fragment of narrative has its own rise and fall and an implicit suspense that is supposed to be relieved (and then continued) twenty-four hours later with the arrival of the next day's paper. But we have placed the next day's episode further down the page.

Read them with that in mind.

And enjoy.

Bill Blackbeard
Martin Williams

I

Struwwelpeter, Pagliacci, and Puss in Boots

Folklore Figures in the Early Sunday Comic Strip, 1896-1916

During its first two decades the new comic-strip medium appeared chiefly on large, pulp paper pages in color-printed Sunday humor and magazine sections of the more prosperous metropolitan newspapers. (Tabloid-size color comic pages first appeared when the *Chicago Tribune, Portland Oregonian,* and other papers introduced them as a paper-saving measure in 1918.) Three comic figures of popular fiction dominated virtually to the exclusion of all others: the demon child, the clownish innocent, and the humanized animal.

And the demon child led all the rest. The character also appeared, in varying degrees of rascality, throughout American fiction at the time the first strips were being conceived, notably with such hellions as Mark Twain's Huckleberry Finn, George W. Peck's Bad Boy, and Edward W. Townsend's Chimmie Fadden. However, he was perhaps even more luridly and seminally rendered in such earlier German popular graphic figures as Heinrich Hoffmann's Struwwelpeter (1845; but anticipated by a figure in Paul Gavarni's illustrations for *Les enfants terribles* of 1843) and Wilhelm Busch's Max and Moritz (1865).

The premier figure of juvenile genius and subversion in the comics was, of course, R. F. Outcault's Yellow Kid. He was almost immediately followed by Rudolph Dirks's longer-lasting Katzenjammer Kids team of Hans and Fritz, which had originally been copied directly from the two *schrecklichkinder* of Busch. Subsequent demon children of the early Sunday comics were Outcault's Buster Brown, Winsor McCay's *Little Sammy Sneeze*, Nemo's troublesome buddies in *Little Nemo in Slumberland*, George McManus's Nibsy (hero of a short-lived spoof on McCay's *Nemo* page, *Nibsy the Newsboy in Funny Fairyland*), James Swinnerton's *Jimmy*, Penny Ross's Esther (in *Mama's Angel Child*), Tad Dorgan's *Johnny Wise*, George Herriman's *Bud Smith*, C. W. Kahles's *Bobby Bounce* (continuing in the strip briefly done in 1902 by W. W. Denslow, illustrator of *The Wizard of Oz*, as *Billy Bounce*), A. C. Fera's Elmer (in

Just Boy), Walter Hoban's *Jerry*, Tom McNamara's city gang in *Us Kids*, Clare Dwiggins's rural kids in *School Days*—and many others.

Almost as common on the early Sunday comic page was the well-meaning, even saintly, fool, who ranged in nineteenth-century literature from Dickens's Mr. Toots in *Dombey and Son* to Dostoevski's Prince Mishkin of *The Idiot*, but who was perhaps most popularly rendered in the sad clown hero of Leoncavallo's later nineteenth-century opera, *I Pagliacci*. Initially introduced to the comic strip in Fred Opper's 1900 Sunday page, *Happy Hooligan*, drawn for Hearst's *New York Journal*, clownish innocents promptly swarmed across the color strips in the guise of such characters as Raymond Ewer's Slim Jim, Billy Marriner's Sambo, Norman R. Jennette's Marseleen (a clown in full Pagliaccian regalia), George McManus's Lovey and Dovey (in *The Newlyweds*), C. M. Payne's Pop (in *S'Matter Pop?*), Rube Goldberg's Boob McNutt, Winsor McCay's Little Nemo, James Swinnerton's Sam (in *Sam and His Laugh*), George Herriman's Major Ozone, Charles Schultz's Foxy Grandpa, and many another.

Not quite as widespread in the early Sunday comics as the two types cited, but a close third in popular usage and appeal, was the humanized animal, found in children's tales and cautionary parables as far back as Aesop, most memorably captured as a prototypical image in Charles Perrault's cocky and adventurous Puss in Boots, and abundantly present in nineteenth-century fiction, notably in Hans Christian Andersen's *Fairy Tales*, the monumental *Scenes in the Private and Public Lives of Animals* by Grandville (J. I. I. Gérard), and Joel Chandler Harris's Uncle Remus series. In the new narrative art of the comic strip, the humanized animal was first introduced by James Swinnerton in the figure of his philandering Mr. Jack, an initially unnamed feline character who first began to emerge as a distinct individual in 1902 in Swinnerton's popularly named *Little Tigers* feature. (Earlier Swinnerton cartoon work featuring anthropomorphized animals, such as his *Little Bears and Tykes* panel of 1893, and his *On and Off the Ark* of circa 1900 and later, did not qualify as definitive comic strips, because of the lack of dialogue balloons and/or individualized and regularly recurrent characters.)

At about the time of Swinnerton's creation of the nattily dressed and highly humanized Mr. Jack, R. F. Outcault, in 1902, was putting salty and sarcastic ripostes in the mouth of Buster Brown's bulldog, Tige, and casually granting speech to other animals in the strip. By 1904 Fred Opper had introduced the demonic, high-kicking Maud the Mule into his cast of comic-page characters—but by then, humanized animals were becoming commonplace in the comics. Among others prominent at the time were Charles Twelvetrees's Johnny Quack and the Van Cluck Twins, Gus Mager's Jungle Folks, the Animal Friends of Walt MacDougall's Hank, J. M. Conde's Uncle Remus characters (Br'er Rabbit *et al.* in *Uncle Remus Stories*), the fantastic animals in Harry Grant Dart's *The Explorigator* and Bob Dean's *Swots*, Sherlock Bones in Lyonel Feininger's *The Kin-der-Kids*, Sidney Smith's *Old Doc Yak*, George Herriman's later *Krazy Kat* (made a Sunday-page figure by 1916), C. M. Payne's *Bear Creek Folks*, and R. K. Culver's *Roosevelt Bears*.

Several of these humanized animal features were not true comic strips; rather, like the currently published *Prince Valiant*, they were lavishly illustrated prose fiction, without balloons or linking panels of action, but their frequency in comic sections of the time and their emphasis on animals speaking intelligently call for their mention here, if not their inclusion in the body of this anthology itself.

Virtually ignored in the Sunday comic pages of these early years was the serious male hero figure, fiercely active in the popular fiction of the time, from Sherlock Holmes to Tarzan. When present at all, he was treated as a butt of satire, notably in F. M. Howarth's *Old Opie Dilldock*, H. A. McGill's daily *Hairbreadth Harold* in Hearst's *New York Journal*, and C. W. Kahles's syndicated *Hairbreadth Harry*.

Women, considered as sympathetic heroines, received little concern until Gene Carr's *Lady Bountiful* appeared as a Sunday page in early 1920, although a few earlier, illustrated-story pages, like Wallace Morgan's *Fluffy Ruffles,* ran in newspapers' Sunday magazine sections, rather than with the comics. Seriously suspenseful narrative continuity, too, was simply nonexistent in these two initial decades between 1896 and 1916, when slapstick humor was the bell-capped, starry-kicked king.

Notes on strips in this section

The strip numbers, in brackets, accompany individual comments as an aid to easy reference.

That's the anticipatory grinning face of George B. Luks looking down on R. F. Outcault's *Hogan's Alley* characters in the opening selection [1]: Luks was to take the *World* feature over from Outcault for Hearst's *Journal* when the latter left, after drawing this final page.

Johnny Wise [2] was a very early page from Tad Dorgan, a cartoonist chiefly noted for his later, daily sports-page strips. It appeared only in the *San Francisco Chronicle.*

The *Little Nemo in Slumberland* episodes [11-14] were selected from McCay's first version of the strip, which ran in the *New York Herald* between 1905 and 1911. (Two subsequent versions ran in other papers. The first appeared in the Hearst papers between 1911 and 1914, and the second in the *New York Herald Tribune* between 1924 and 1927. Examples of pages from these two later versions will be found in the third section of this book.)

The appearance of Lyonel Feininger's remarkable *Kin-der-Kids* [16-18] page in the *Chicago Tribune* in 1906 marked the first occasion of a regularly appearing comic strip being drawn and imported from abroad; in this instance, from Germany. Editorial difficulties arising from this procedure led to the strip's demise in less than a year.

Johnny Gruelle, creator of the charming fairyland fantasy *Mr. Twee Deedle* [20], later, of course, wrote the Raggedy Ann book series.

C. M. Payne's *Bear Creek Folks* [24-25] was derived in part from Albert Bigelow Paine's *Hollow Tree* book series with their striking J. M. Conde illustrations, and more remotely from Joel Chandler Harris's Uncle Remus stories, but it often reads like an anticipation of Walt Kelly's later *Pogo.*

Clare Victor Dwiggins's *School Days* [26-27] is notable (aside from its art and wacky humor) as having been the first strip to feature the screwball devices or "inventions," with which Rube Goldberg later became identified.

The *Mutt and Jeff* Sunday pages reproduced here were among the first to be released in color, but they are typical of the earlier Sunday black and white pages published in the Hearst press circa 1911-1913, and reflect the inspired slapstick qualities which made Bud Fisher's team one of the great strip hits of all time. [28-29]

Gus Mager's *Hawkshaw the Detective* [31] was the Sunday-page continuation of his earlier daily strip, *Sherlocko the Monk.* Originally supposed to be called *Sherlocko the Detective,* the Sunday page was retitled *Hawkshaw* (borrowing the name of the detective once famed in Tom Taylor's melodramatic play of 1863, *The Ticket-of-Leave Man*)—with the name of Sherlocko's associate, Watso, changed to the Colonel—because of threatened suit by A. Conan Doyle's American representatives for titular infringement of Doyle's Sherlock Holmes and Dr. Watson characters.

[1]

OPENING OF THE HOGAN'S ALLEY ATHLETIC CLUB.

[3]

© American-Journal-Examiner, 1905

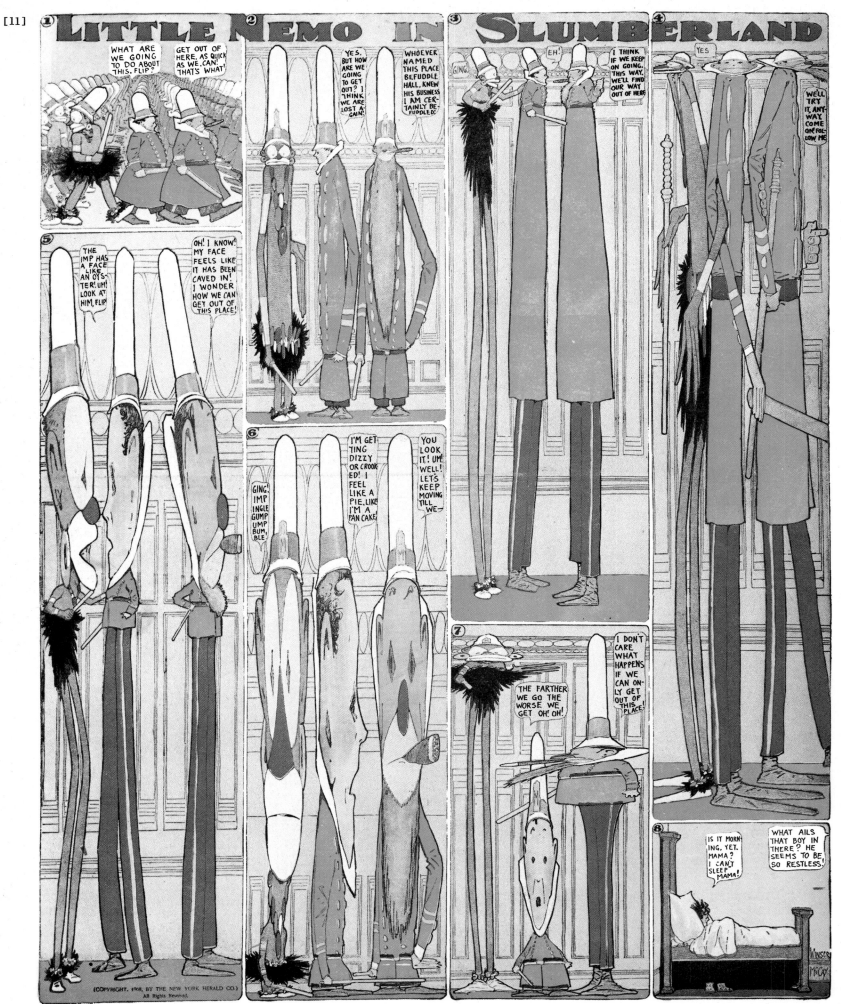

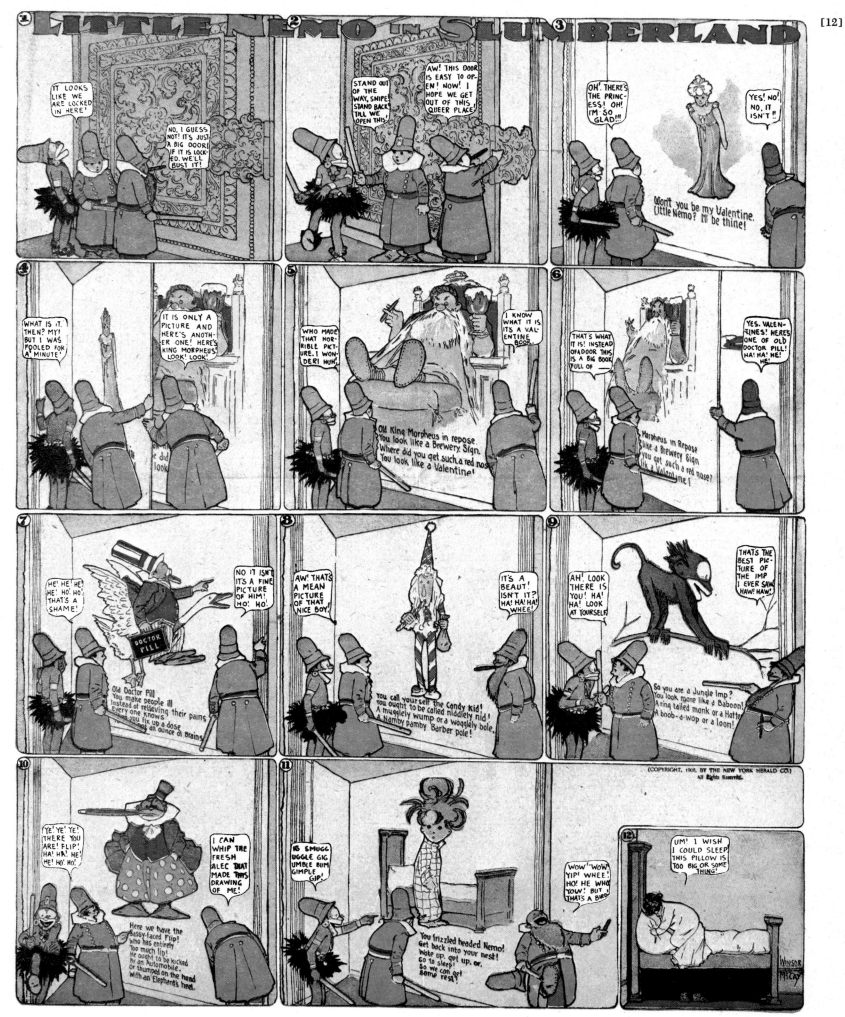

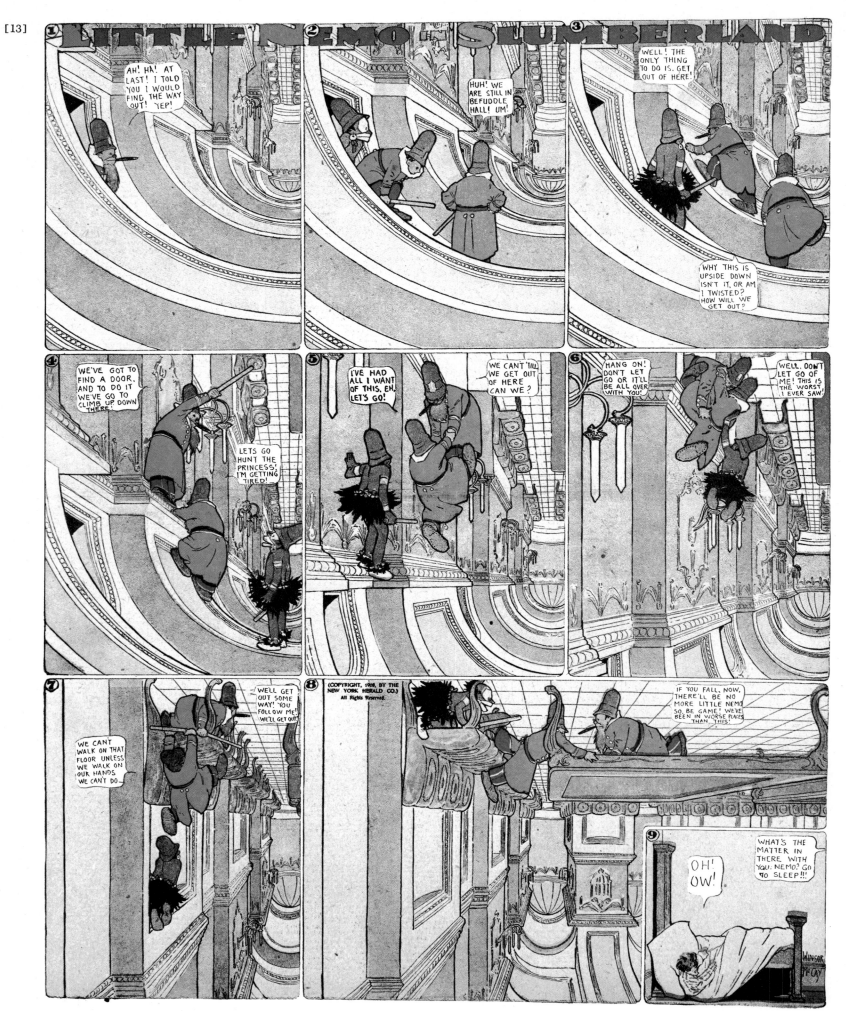

[15]

MR·TWEE·DEEDLE·

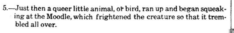

1.—After their escape from the angry owner of the lake, the friends came upon a queer looking tuft of grass with eight flowers growing from it. "It looks like a porcupine," said Mr. Twee Deedle; "we'd better not disturb it."

2.—But the Moon Man paid no attention and picked two of the flowers. The tuft of grass rose slowly from the ground. "The flowers are made of cloth," cried the Moon Man.

3.—The grass was followed by a long, slim body with mournful eyes which turned reproachfully on the Moon Man and seemed to hypnotize him so he could not run.

4.—"How dare you disturb the King of the Mirage Moodles?" cried the strange creature, as it leaned toward the Moon Man. He could not run, but Dickie and Mr. Twee Deedle began to throw stones at the Moodle.

5.—Just then a queer little animal, or bird, ran up and began squeaking at the Moodle, which frightened the creature so that it trembled all over.

6.—The bird-beast pecked at the Moodle and drove it back into the ground, but they didn't notice another Moodle rising from the ground behind them.

7.—In a few moments the little group was completely surrounded by Moodles. "Squeak," the bird-beast told them and they all began to cry "Squeak" together with six little bird-beasts which had joined them. As the Moodles began to go back into the ground they punctured them and let the gas escape.

8.—The bird-beasts marched off and the friends went to find the Rubber Man to get some cement in order to mend the Moodles.

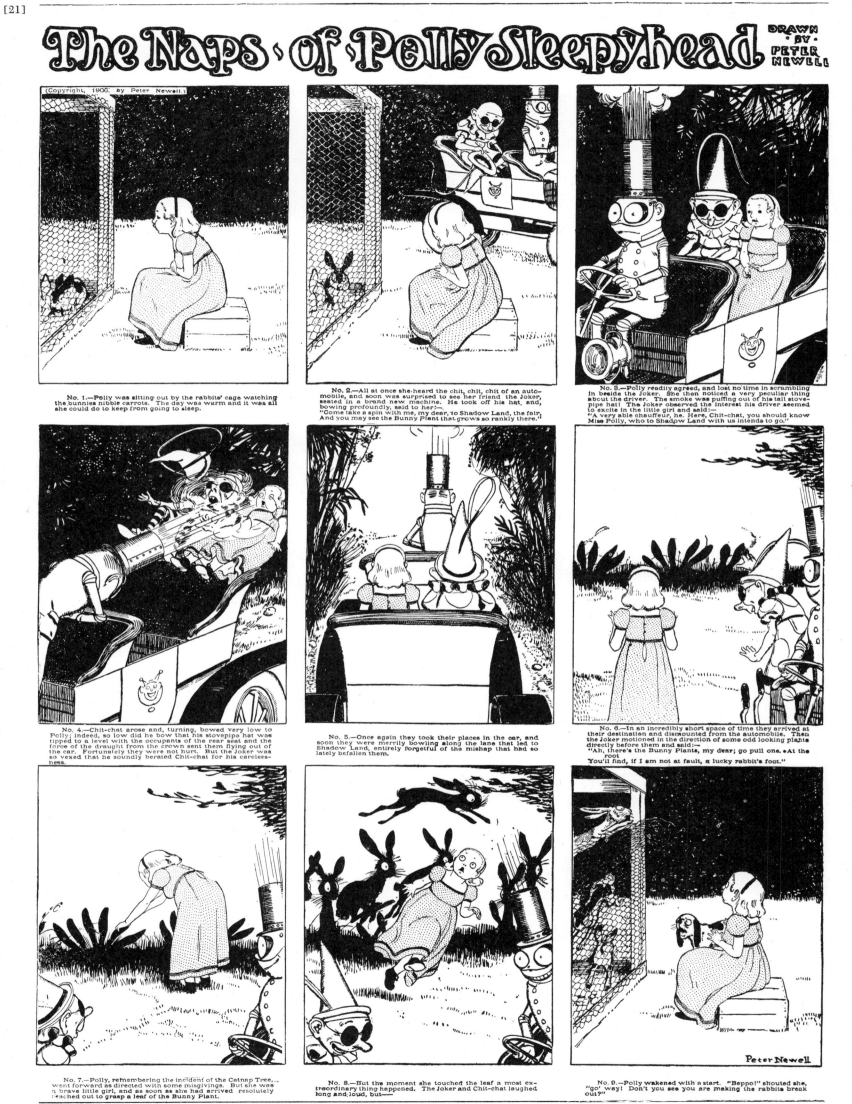

© Peter Newell, 1906

[23]

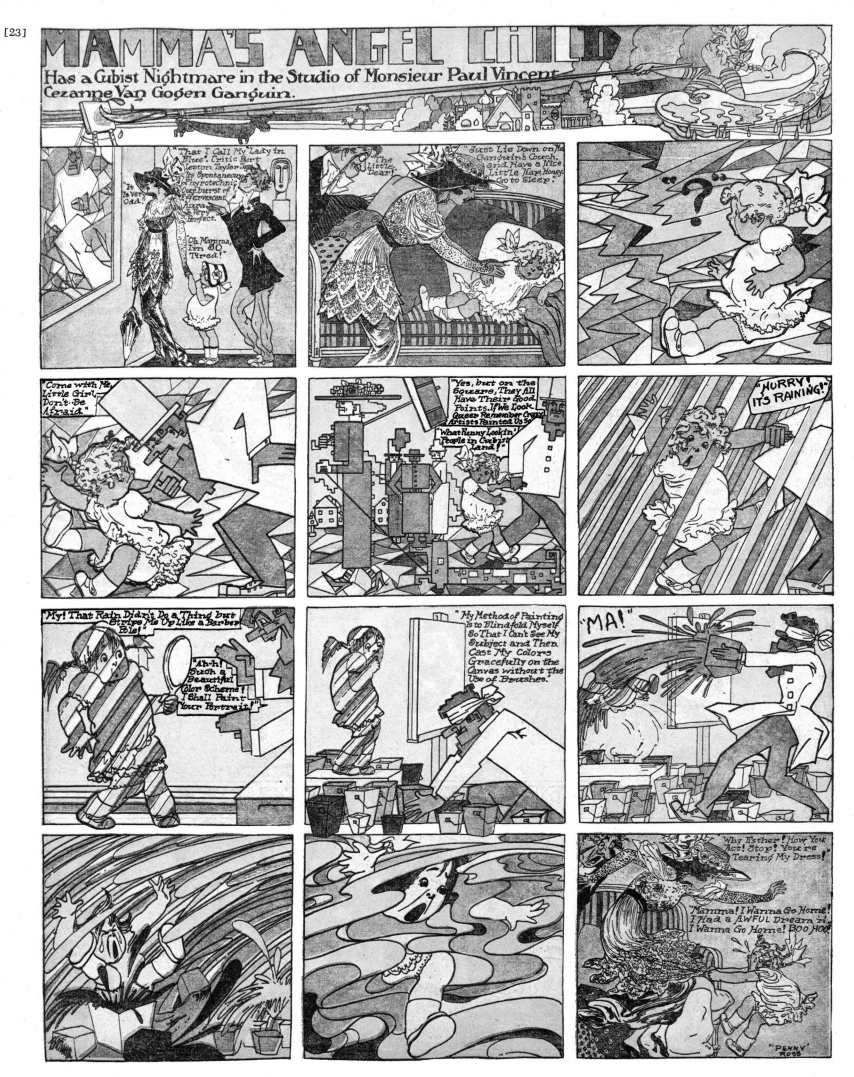

[26]

[27]

© H. C. Fisher, 1918

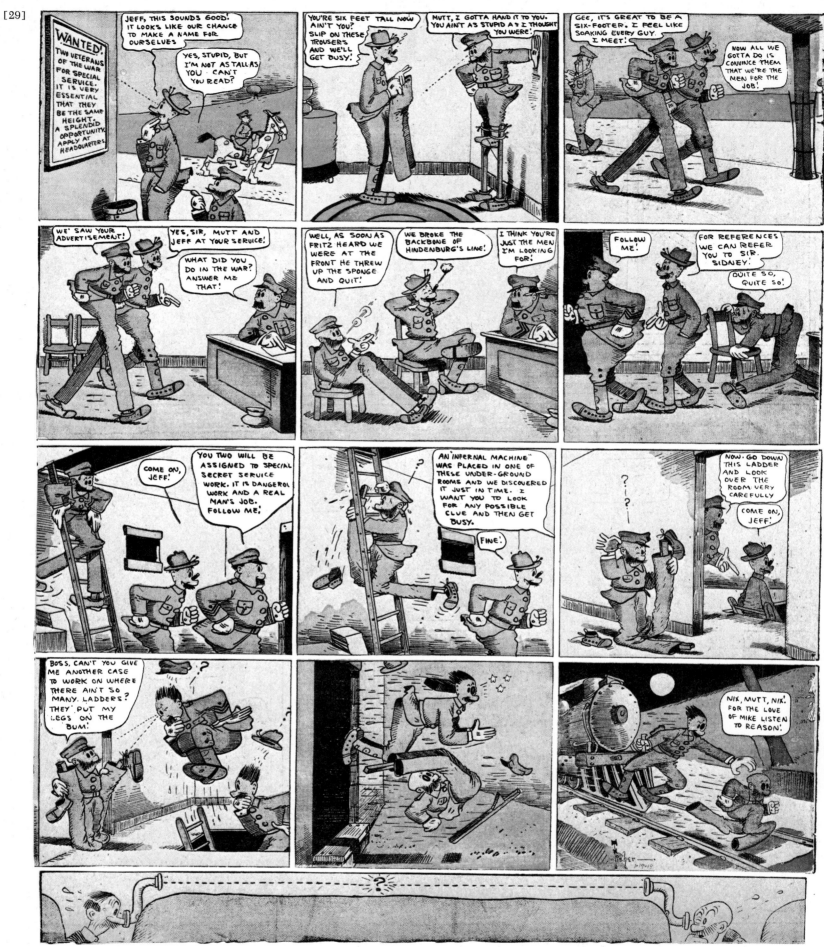

© H. C. Fisher, 1919

[31]

Hawkshaw the Detective---The Colonel Is a Little Too Hasty

II

Mr. Caudle,
Sherlock Holmes,
and the Artless Dodger

Popular Images in the

Early Daily Comic Strip,

1907-1927

Comic strips in their definitive form did not appear in weekday newspapers until the turn of the century, when the Hearst dailies began to feature recurrent cartoon characters in black and white, multipanel gag sequences. Some were in an illustrated text format, but most were in true comic strip style of four to six panels per sequence. At first they were drawn by Hearst staff cartoonists in New York and mailed to the other papers; later, some were created locally. None, however, appeared regularly every day, Monday through Saturday, until Bud Fisher began his *A. Mutt* strip in 1907.

These early and irregular Hearst weekday strips, a group of which are reproduced on the first page of this section, were aimed more at adult readers than were most of the early Sunday comics, and their characters and attitudes were therefore different from those of the weekend color pages. This relatively sophisticated orientation was retained for the daily strip as its use spread among newspapers and the strips added three additional figures of popular lore—the henpecked father, the omniscient detective, and the luckless, therefore lovable, scalawag.

Married figures had already appeared in the color strips, of course, but virtually all of these fell into the innocent fool category (*The Newlyweds, Their Only Child, S'Matter Pop?* and so forth), while the prototypical image of the henpecked husband (with its countervailing image of the domineering wife), which was to be so widely utilized in the early weekday strips, appeared only indirectly in the early Sunday pages, in the form of the rolling-pin-belabored Captain in Dirks's *Katzenjammer Kids,* who was not married to the Kids' often irate mother, but was her star boarder. The classic figure of the wife-beset, but cynically struggling, husband was portrayed often and well by Dickens, particularly in his rendition of the paterfamilial worm in Mr. Snagsby of *Bleak House* and the foredoomed Captain Cuttle of *Dombey and Son,* but he was perhaps most memorably set forth in popular nineteenth-century fiction as Douglas Jerrold's vocally berated hero of *Mrs. Caudle's Curtain Lectures* in 1865. He appeared notably for the first time in strips as Gus Mager's Henpecko the Monk, in the weekday strip of the same name, circa 1908. Two years later, George Herriman introduced E. Pluribus Dingbat in his *Dingbat Family,* followed in the strips by a number of similarly browbeaten breadwinners.

George McManus combined the hapless husband image with that of the socially rising family (a theme long treated satirically in popular American literature and drama) in his daily *Bringing Up Father* strip of 1914 in the Hearst papers. McManus's Jiggs was an Irish bricklayer-become-millionaire, Maggie was an ambitious virago of a wife, and after their appearance, henpeckery became a stock subject in the daily strips (broadening later into the Sunday pages): Sidney Smith's *The Gumps,* Billy De Beck's *Barney Google,* Gene Ahern's *Our Boarding House,* Harry Tuthill's *Home, Sweet Home* (later *The Bungle Family*), A. D. Condo's *The Outbursts of Everett True,* Cliff Sterrett's *Polly and Her Pals,* Bud Fisher's *Mutt and Jeff,* W. R. Allman's *Doings of the Duffs,* and many more.

The all-perceptive detective, a mythic figure essentially developed in nineteenth-century fiction and drama (the term itself only dates from 1843, when Sir James Graham, British Home Secretary, coined it in forming his "Detective Police," a body made up of the most intelligent London police officers of the time), was first effectively introduced to popular literature as a figure of detached, analytical intellect in Edgar Allan Poe's C. Auguste Dupin of "The Murders in the Rue Morgue" (1841) and as an image of dogged strength and hard-boiled professionalism in Charles Dickens's Inspector Bucket of *Bleak House* (1853). But it was A. Conan Doyle who, in his *A Study In Scarlet* of 1887, combined brain with cold professionalism and strong personality in a classic version of the fictional sleuth Sherlock Holmes. The Holmes concept spread like paper-fed fire through popular literature during the following decades and reached the comic strip in a short-lived Hearst weekday spoof of 1904 called *Padlock Bones,* by H. A. McGill.

Burlesques of Holmes followed in other strips, both daily and Sunday, but the detective's most famous early strip avatar was Gus Mager's weekday Sherlocko the Monk, who first appeared in the strip of that name in Hearst's *New York Journal* for December 9, 1910, later to become even better known as Hawkshaw the Detective. The Holmes character was burlesqued further in Sidney Smith's early Sunday *Sherlock Holmes, Jr.* for the *Chicago Tribune,* and as a comic figure in such established strips as Dirks's *Katzenjammer Kids,* which featured an Eskimo detective named Sherlock Gunk, and Segar's in *Thimble Theatre,* which involved a Gimlet the Detective and a Shamrock Jones in its daily continuity. More generalized detective figures appeared elsewhere, as in Harry Hershfield's weekday *Dauntless Durham of the U. S. A.* and Sidney Smith's daily *Buck Nix.*

The third and perhaps most widespread new figure in the daily comic strip was the inept but charming rogue. He had long been a figure in popular literature, of course, notably as Falstaff, or (more recently) as Dickens's Seth Pecksniff in *Martin Chuzzlewit,* or Mark Twain's King and the Duke in *Huckleberry Finn,* or in the more heroically presented Tom and Jerry of Pierce Egan's *Life in London* and Sut Lovingood of George W. Harris's American fables. This image had appeared in the early Sunday pages, but almost always as either a subsidiary character (i.e., Long John Silver in Dirks's *Katzenjammer Kids,* or Rudolph Rassendale in Kahles's *Hairbreadth Harry*), or as one or more titular figures whose roguery was implicit, in dress and manner, rather than explicit in behavior (i.e., Alphonse and Gaston, in Opper's strip of that name, or Tom and Jerry in Rube Goldberg's early *The Look-a-Like Boys*). The one notable exception was Swinnerton's married flirt in *Mr. Jack* (whose weekly strip behavior in pages read by children upset many readers and led to the strip's being relegated to infrequent daily appearance in the safe, smoking-room atmosphere of the sports and editorial pages after 1904). But in the daily strips, with their essentially adult audience at the time, scurvy vagabondage prospered. Artless Dodgers were memorable in such early daily strips as Bud Fisher's *Mutt and Jeff*, Clare Briggs's *A. Piker Clerk*, Gus Mager's various conniving Monks (excepting Sherlocko, of course), George Herriman's *Baron Bean*, Dok Hager's *Dippy Duck*, Sidney Smith's *Buck Nix* and *Old Doc Yak*, Billy De Beck's *Barney Google*, Frank Willard's *Moon Mullins*, E. C. Segar's *Thimble Theatre*, Harry Hershfield's *Desperate Desmond* and *Abie the Agent,* and many, many more.

The order of the day in daily strips between 1907 and 1927 was satire, cheerful cynicism, and subdued slapstick, centered on helpless husbands, burlesque detectives, and inept scoundrels. But new kinds of strips and heroes did enter the scene in the 1920s and shape the character of all strips in the following decade.

For instance, the image of the self-reliant working girl in an office background enjoyed its most extensive use in the daily strips, and developed in the 1920s in such strips as *Tillie the Toiler* and *Somebody's Stenog;* it was not a part of the group of prototypical figures which shaped much of the content of the initial daily strip work.

Notes on strips in this section

Gus Mager's Monk strips [34, 36] ran initially under a number of alternative titles, reflecting the name of the character featured in a given episode: *Tightwaddo the Monk, Knocko the Monk, Nervo the Monk,* and so on. Their popularity inspired the stage names given to four of the Marx Brothers during a poker game, and the team used them during the rest of their career.

The *Desperate Desmond* [37] strip was named for its top-hatted villain protagonist; the opposing hero was named Claude Eclair, and the heroine Fair Rosamond. The prose narrative under each panel was auxiliary rather than explanatory, making the feature an odd combination of illustrated fiction and comic strip.

Midsummer Day Dreams [40], the Winsor McCay work, is typical of a large number of daily graphic anecdotes he drew at this time. Few, if any, involved repeated characters, and no comic strip developed out of them.

The *A. Mutt* episodes included here [41-46] ran only in the *San Francisco Examiner* of the time (Bud Fisher having been hired away from the *Chronicle* by that paper in 1907) and involve the first appearance of Mutt's later partner, Jeff. The casual comic use of a lunatic asylum as the setting is typical of the irreverent, freewheeling content of the early daily strips.

The Family Upstairs [48-53], first named *The Dingbat Family,* and later given that name again, carried the earliest exploits of Herriman's Krazy Kat krew, at first around the feet of the human cast of the strip, and then in a separate row of panels below them. The "family upstairs" of the title refers to a mysterious menage living in the apartment above that of the Dingbats, none of whose members are ever seen in the strip, and whose weird doings drive the Dingbats to a frenzy of curiosity and animosity.

Baron Bean [54-77] featured a pretentious, ragtag bum of similar mien to Dicken's Montague Tigg/Tigg Montague of *Martin Chuzzlewit,* who was often at fanciful war with his strangely loyal manservant, Grimes.

Stumble Inn [78-83] was an extraordinarily lavish daily strip of the dimensions indicated in the selections here. Short-lived as a daily, it ran for several years as a Sunday page and exhibited Herriman's fancy in a somewhat more restrained context than usual.

Dok's Dippy Duck [84-91] was the strip-in-residence of the *Seattle Times,* appearing only in that paper and running seven days a week, either on the front page or just inside. The resemblance of the cocky Dippy to the later Disney Donald Duck is self-evident, reflecting a common human perception of the nature of ducks.

Buck Nix [92-95] first appeared as a strip outgrowth of the sidelines master of ceremonies to Sidney Smith's *Chicago American* sports-page cartoons, which displayed Smith's comic genius as an absorbing storyteller. An audience quickly developed which preferred *Buck Nix* to more formal sports art. Hired away by the *Chicago Tri-*

bune, Smith continued Buck as *Old Doc Yak* [103-107], first as a Sunday page, then briefly as a daily in order to introduce Smith's new strip concept, *The Gumps* [96-102].

The second group of Bud Fisher episodes selected are a random potpourri of *Mutt and Jeff* [108-125] from its best period in the late 1920s and early 1930s.

The reader will note the descriptive phrases and subheads assigned to the early strips in this section. As strips became more and more popular, and more and more widely syndicated, the composition and addition of a daily descriptive subhead gradually became the prerogative of the comics editor of each subscribing local paper, not that of the author or the syndicate's own editor. Accordingly, we have dropped the subheads from most of the daily episodes which follow in this volume.

Mr. Jack   James Swinnerton   1904

Mr. E. Z. Mark   F. M. Howarth   1907

[32]

[33]

He Can't Keep From Bragging, Even in His Sleep.

© American-Journal-Examiner, 1907

They Steal a March on the Star Boarder.

© American-Journal-Examiner, 1907

The funny paper has . . . become not only a faithful reflection of the tastes and ethical principles of the country at large; it is also manifestly an extremely powerful organ of social satire. The daily block of cinema-squares is the medium through which the vices of man are held up for all to see . . . . The few cardinal virtues that we sometimes venture apologetically to call our own are disregarded by the funnies as comparatively uninteresting to the non-church-goer, and as 'old stuff' to the veteran of the Sunday-school bench or the straight-backed pew. All of them, it is true, draw largely on contemporary manners for their subject matter, but the genuine masterpieces of the art use these merely as machinery for the display of the essential Satan, the unquenchable 'Peck's Bad Boy,' in all of us.

Ernest Brennecke
"The Real Mission of the Funny Paper," Century Magazine, March 1924.

[36]

[37]

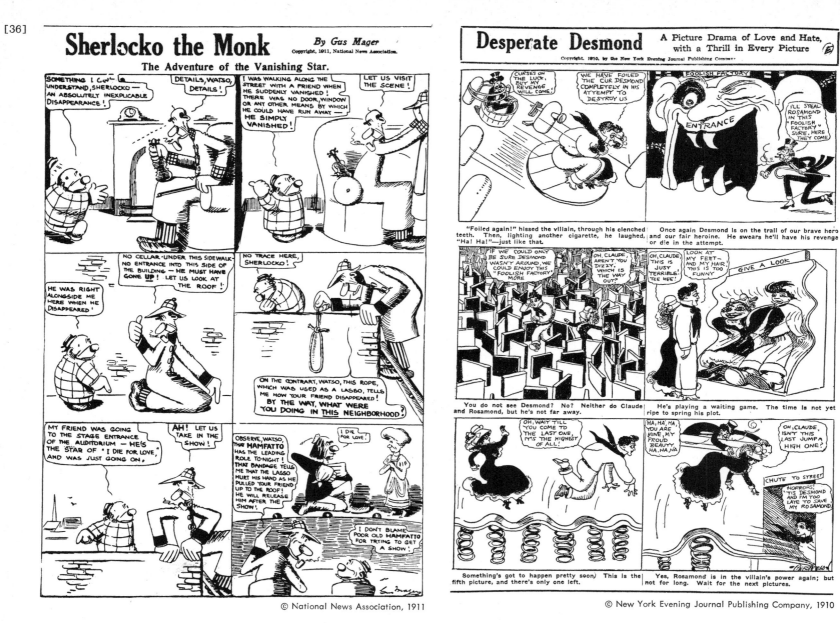

© National News Association, 1911

© New York Evening Journal Publishing Company, 1910

Chantecler Peck   F. G. Long   1911

S'Matter Pop?   Charles M. Payne   1911

[38]

[39]

© Press Publishing Co. (The New York World), 1911

© Press Publishing Co. (The New York World), 1911

Midsummer Day Dreams

Copyright, 1911, by the National News Association

By WINSOR M'CAY

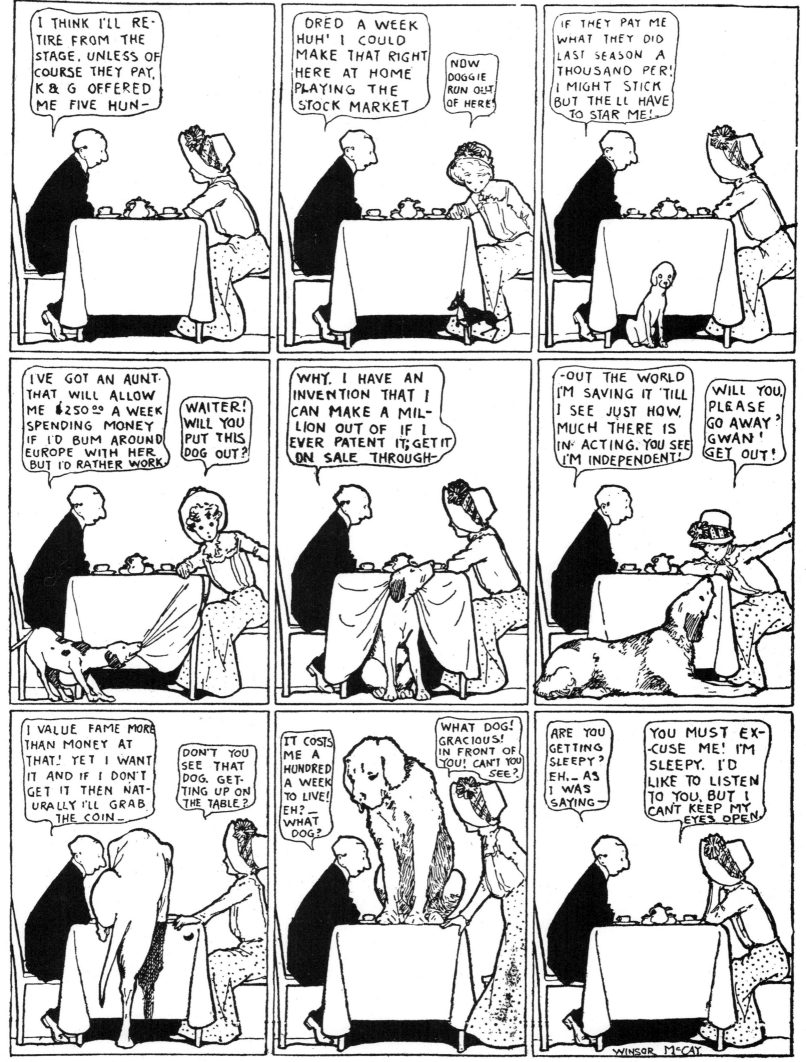

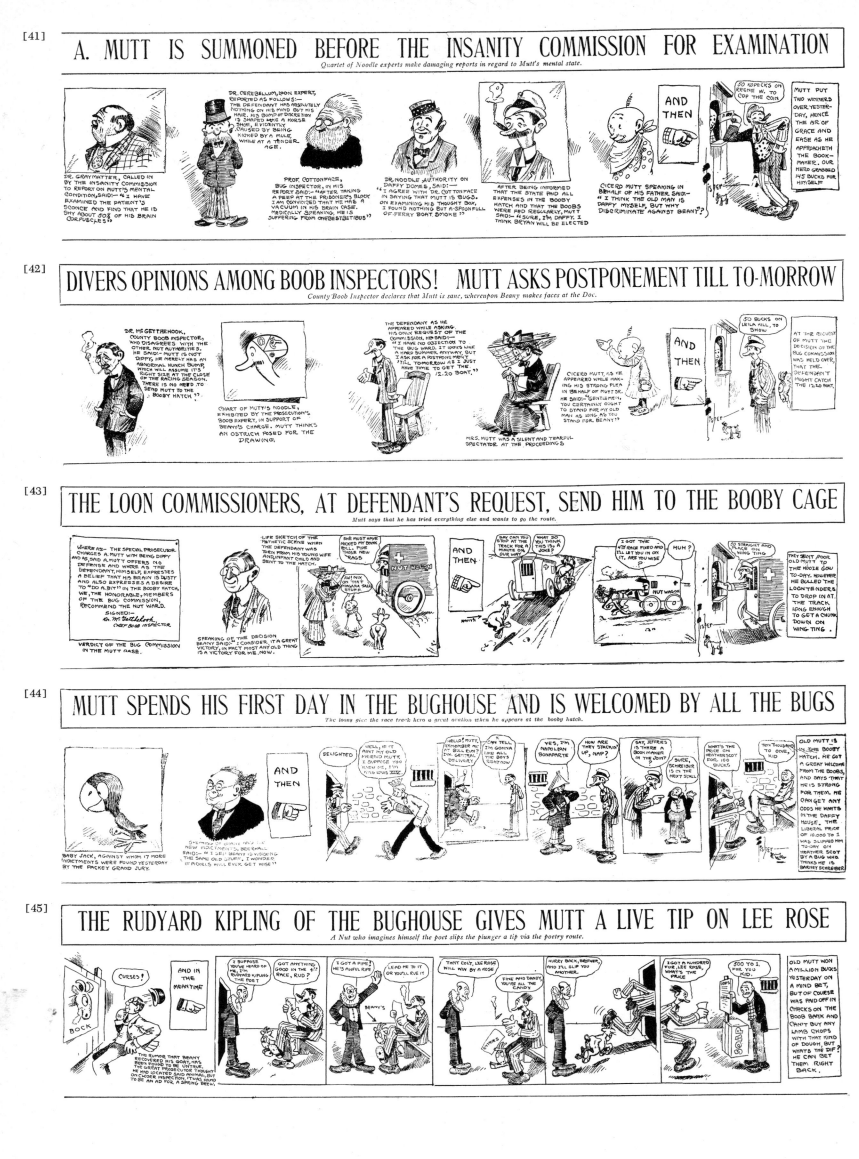

EFFORT BEING MADE TO HAVE CITY PAY FUTURE EXPENSES OF GREAT MUTT CASE
Many Think This Indicates That Beany Has Lost His Grip on Pickels.

A. Piker Clerk   Clare Briggs   1904

A. PIKER CLERK COMES TO THE RESCUE OF CHICAGO WITH A TIP ON THE RACES---KITTY CLYDE TO WIN.

A. Piker is avowedly a generous man. He hears of Mayor Harrison's worry over the lack of finances to run the city properly. He plunges into the breach. "Kitty Clyde to win," he whispers. The Mayor sees a ray of hope. "Take this," he says as he hands the municipal bag to A. Piker. Off to the bookmaker goes our hero. See to-day's race results.

The Family Upstairs   George Herriman   1911

[49]

[50]

[51]

[52]

Baron Bean   George Herriman   1917

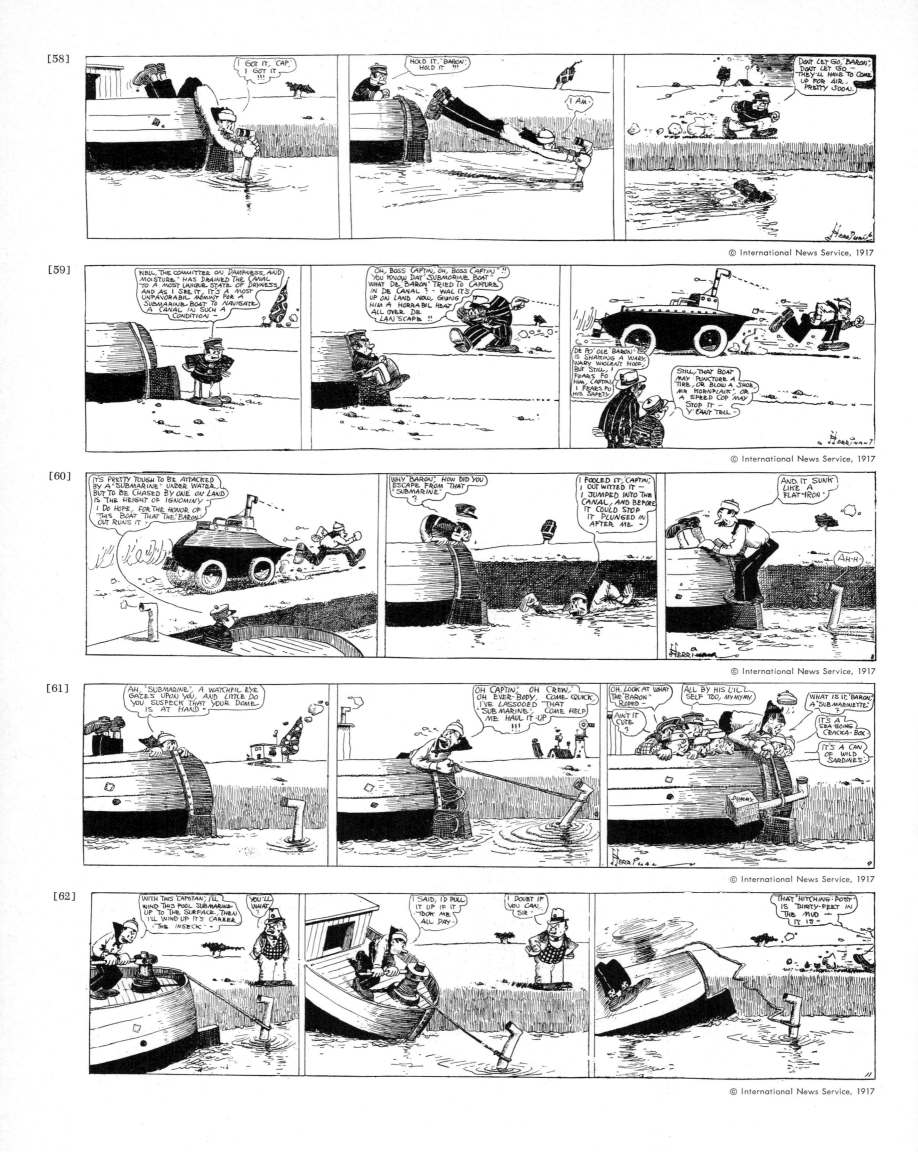

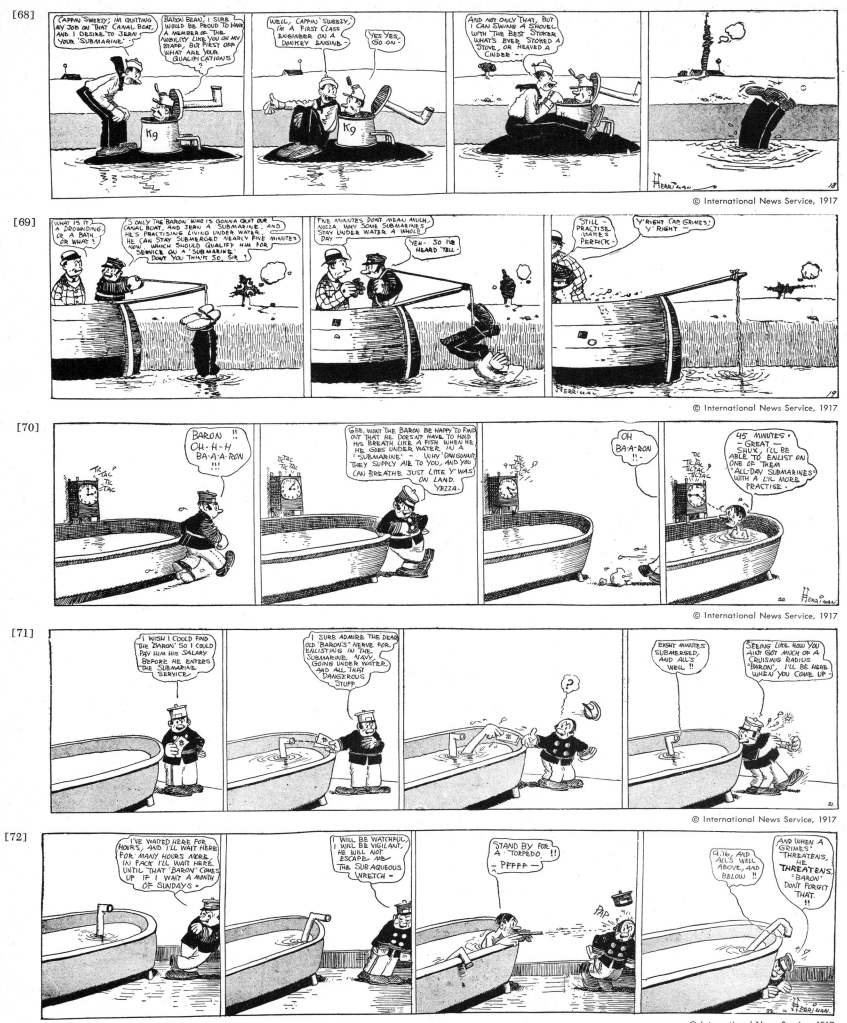

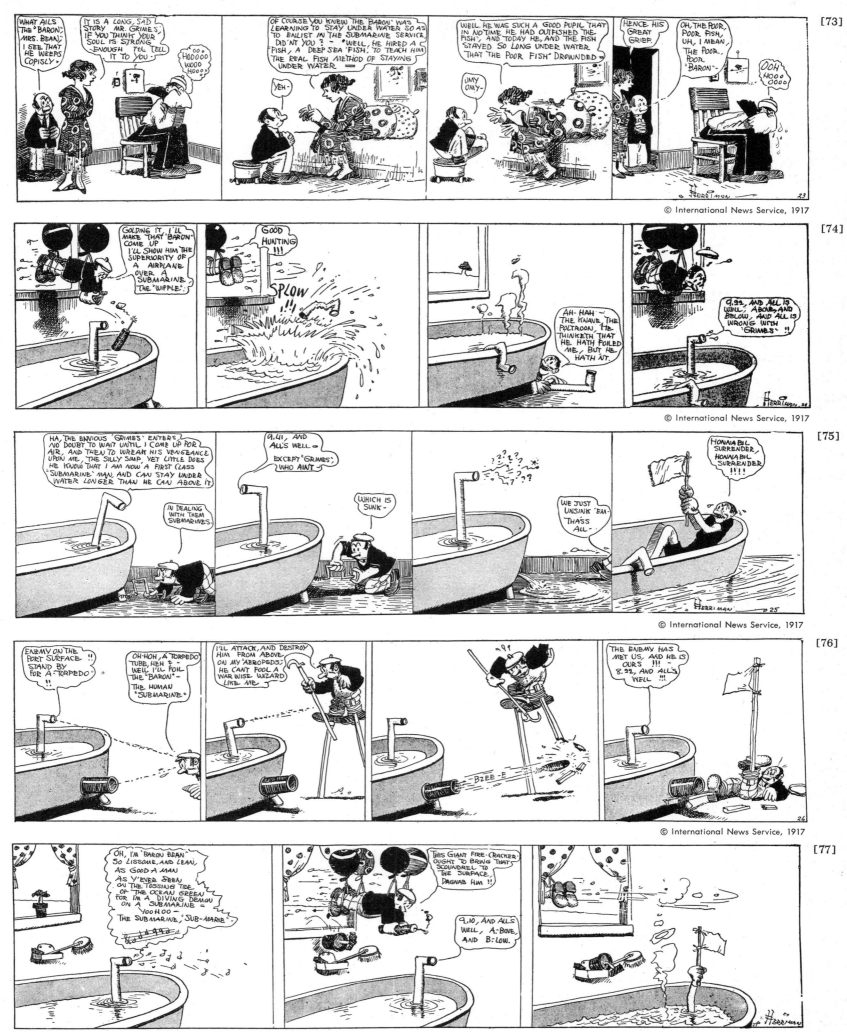

[84]   [85]   [86]   [87]

[88]   [89]   [90]   [91]

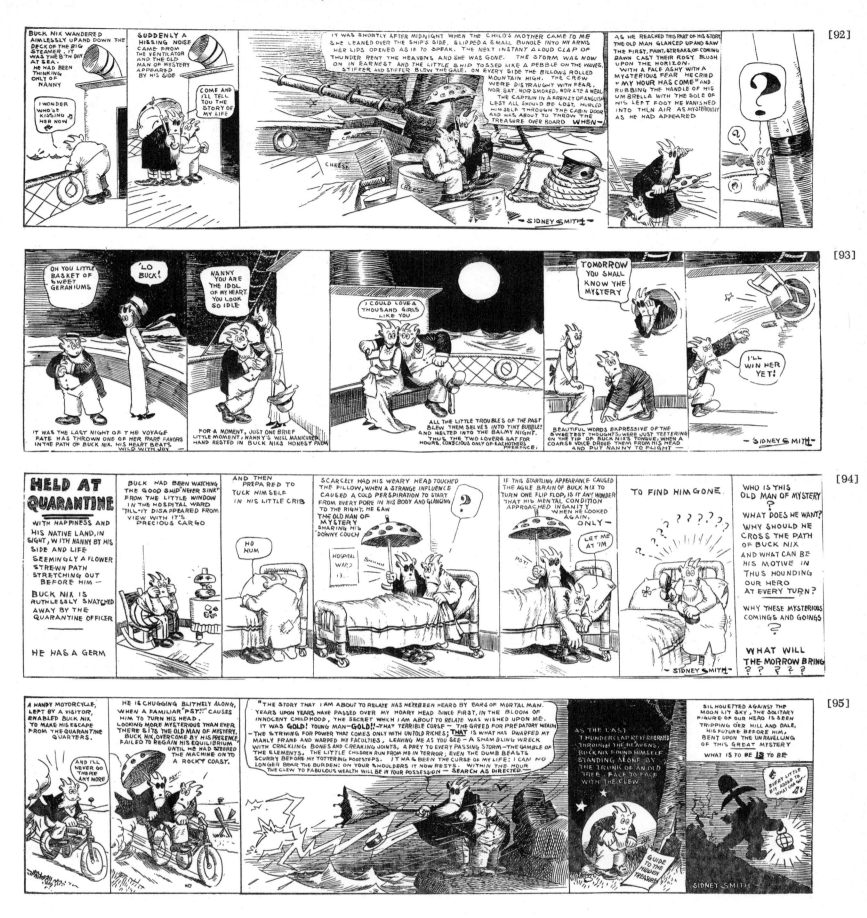

Old Doc Yak   Sidney Smith   1917 (precedes *The Gumps* in date)

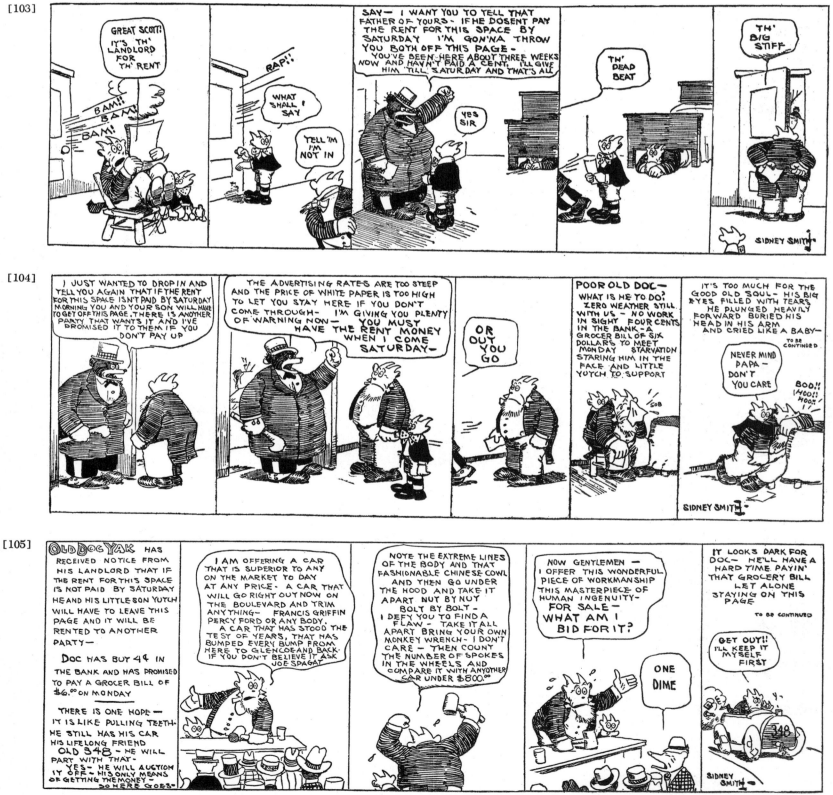

Mutt and Jeff   H. C. "Bud" Fisher   1927 / 1928 / 1932

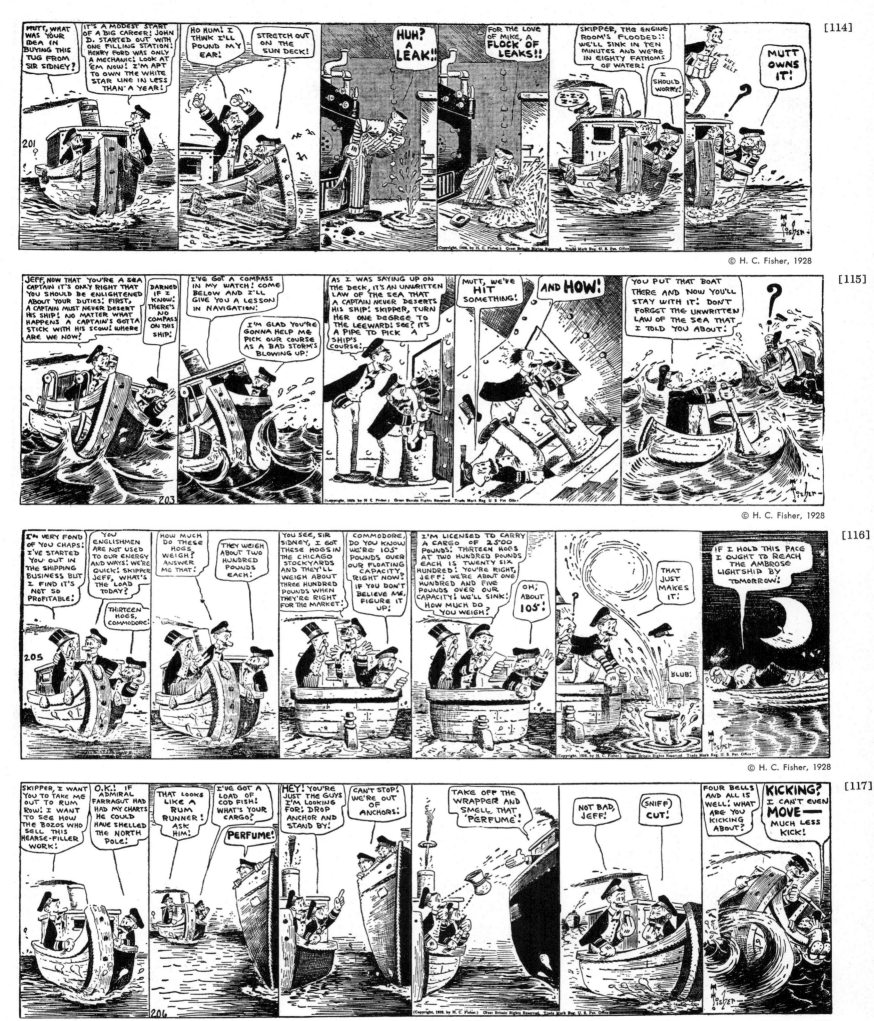

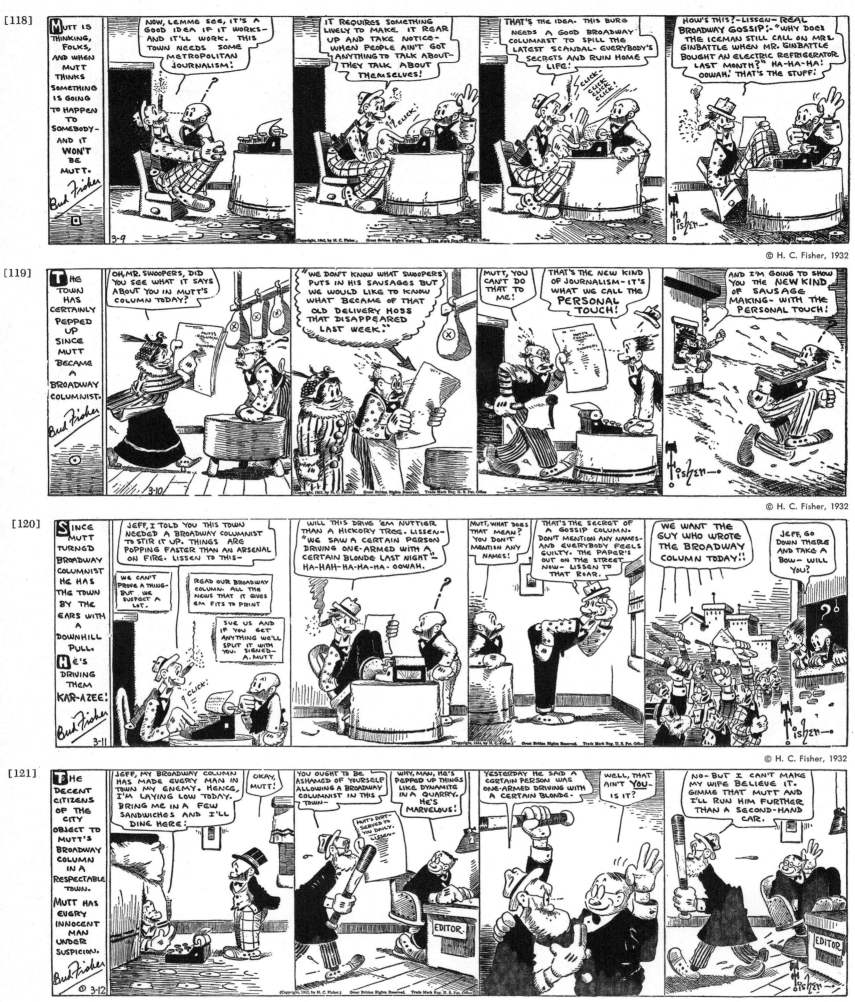

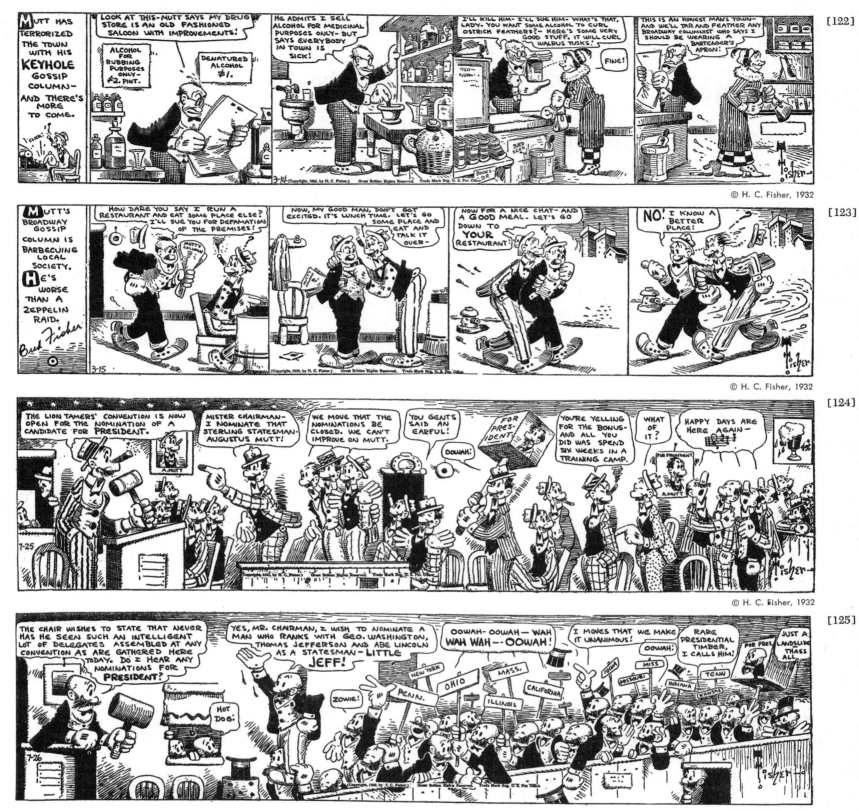

I have that fallacious feeling of absolute knowledge that a first edition of Theodore Dreiser will have only the value of its covers for a quaint period chocolate box in 2000 A.D., whereas the single copy known of three famous comic strips, say 'Mutt and Jeff,' 'Andy Gump,' and 'Krazy Kat,' complete from their beginnings, cut out and pasted in endless oilcloth-covered volumes by an invalid spinster of the epoch on an isolated farm, will have something like the value of the original manuscript, say, of the Book of the Dead.

William Bolitho
"Comic Strip," Camera Obscura, 1930

III

Old Cunning Stagers

Long-Lived Stars of the

Comic Strip's Second Two Decades

1916-1936

This section of Sunday pages is devoted to famous and long-surviving characters brought to life in the multitude of comic strips which packed the color comic sections of the 1920s and early 1930s.

That was the period in which weekend comic sections went from four to eight and then to sixteen pages, with the Hearst papers initiating a fantastic thirty-two-page tabloid section in 1935. And that encouraged the proliferation of new strips from the dozen or more syndicates which were by then supplying an insatiable newspaper market. The old and established strips seemed to retain their earlier places through the floodtide of new titles, and a few of the new strips (*Moon Mullins* and others) displayed the qualities necessary to match the audiences for the classic works, and to continue through the subsequent decades with them. We have included a short-lived but very typical new strip of the period, *The Smythes*.

This was also the last great period of full Sunday pages for each and every strip. In the 1940s half pages and even one-third pages for major strips gradually became a common and accepted thing. The galaxy of the comic strip never again was to glow so brightly as during these last marvelous years of its springtide.

Notes on strips in this section   *The Smythes* [126-127] represents one of the few occasions (but not the only) in which one of the circle of *New Yorker* magazine panel cartoonists ventured into the comic strip. Rea Irvin, the strip's creator, did these Sunday pages for the *New York Herald Tribune*, whose comic section was marked by a special sophistication and restraint.

The *Gumps* pages included [128-129] are typical of this immensely popular strip of the 1920s, whose saucy familial banter and obsession with cars suited the public's fancy. The "Old 348," Andy Gump's large-licensed auto, was inherited by him from Sidney Smith's previous Sunday-page hero, Old Doc Yak.

Cliff Sterrett was, after George Herriman, the unbridled and unflagging graphic master of the comic Sunday page. In fact, Sterrett took his popular strip of family life so far from formal graphic reality that his syndicate became alarmed and ordered him to restore some measure of comprehensive normality before his readership abandoned him in the same perplexity with which they reacted to Herriman's *Krazy Kat*. The pages of *Polly and Her Pals* reproduced here only suggest the extent of Sterrett's brilliant graphic work in the late 1920s [130-135].

These later *Moon Mullins* Sunday pages [138-139] are concerned with the first appearance in the strip of Moon's earthy Uncle Willie, an event roughly similar to the first tentative introduction of Mrs. Gamp into Dickens's *Martin Chuzzlewit*.

This second group of McCay's *Nemo* pages [140-142] combines examples from the strip's second Hearst period (the first two selections of 1912) and its third and final period with the *Herald Tribune* (the last selection of 1925). As can be seen, McCay's imagination did not flag, although his graphic verve was hampered by the *Herald Tribune's* policy of a standard twelve-panel format for most of his later work.

The unforgettable images of C. W. Kahles's delightful cast of melodramatic characters are shown to advantage in this example of *Hairbreadth Harry* [143] from Kahles's last decade as a cartoonist.

In the mastery of strip graphics, few cartoonists have equaled George McManus, as these two selections of his *Bringing Up Father* will demonstrate [144-145]. The humor he sustained over the years in developing the familial conflict between Jiggs and Maggie is also well evidenced.

Included here are the *Katzenjammer Kids* pages of Harold H. Knerr [146-148], drawn for the Hearst papers from the mid-1910s on, after Rudolph Dirks left Hearst to continue his strip elsewhere, and now called *The Captain and the Kids*. Both Dirks and Knerr have their partisans, but they were both ingenious in handling the Katzenjammer menage.

Barney Google [149-150], the rogue and vagabond strip *ne plus ultra*, along with Frank Willard's equally perceptive *Moon Mullins* [138-139], caught the raffish, desperate, yet raucously colorful quality of lower-class, pool-hall-and-race-track life of the twenties. Billy De Beck even extended the scope of his strip to the expatriate Paris of Hemingway and Fitzgerald, as will be noted in one of the selections included here. De Beck's later turn to backwoods hillbilly life with the introduction of Snuffy Smith in the early thirties probably resulted from his own distaste for the grim decade which replaced the roisterous twenties, and his attempt to find an idyllic world to replace it.

Frank King had a highly fanciful way with his Sunday-page work which is often overlooked in discussions of his cradle-to-maturity family saga, *Gasoline Alley*, featuring Uncle Walt and Skeezix. Here we have reproduced some of King's finest pages [151-156], including one which mildly parodies German expressionism, one which brings the look of woodcuts to the comic strip, and others which startlingly follow the twelve-panel progress of the characters across a full-page field of static background.

Rube Goldberg's *Boob McNutt* [157-158] was one of the few major narrative and suspense strips which never appeared in a daily format, running from start to finish as a Sunday page only. The two examples shown here are from the strip's earlier, anecdotal phase.

Merely Margy [161] was the comic strip of John Held, Jr., renowned artist for *College Humor* and other youthfully oriented publications of the period. Like most of Held's popular work, *Margy* reflected the view of college and "flapper" life held by most collegiate youths of the time, from coonskin coats to hip flasks.

Somebody's Stenog [162] was a Sunday page of fine graphic verve, a point which has sadly been lost because of the feature's later reputation as a kind of second-string *Tillie the Toiler*.

Harry Tuthill was the Louis-Ferdinand Céline of the comic page, and his bleakly jaundiced view of lower-middle-class family life (happily offset by a wild sense of humor and a fancy which filled the later strips with gnomes, enchanted mice, fairies, magicians, and time-travel) is well reflected in the group of early 1930s *Bungle Family* pages reprinted here [163-169].

George Herriman's *Krazy Kat*, the apogee of comic-strip art and narrative to date, puzzled so much of the readership of its time that many Hearst chain editors published the Sunday pages only under direct orders from Hearst himself, who recognized and appreciated Herriman's fey genius. However, Hearst had it printed in the weekly drama and arts section of his papers, where it had to run in black and white, rather than in the full panoply of color which Herriman could put to the stunning use demonstrated in Section Seven of this collection. Virtually all of Herriman's Sunday-page work between 1916 and 1934 accordingly ran in black and white (except for a brief group of pages published in the *New York Journal* in 1922) and the preponderance is reflected in the selection reproduced here [170-172].

The *Blondie* page is typical of the early strips [173].

Our *Skippy* selection demonstrates Percy Crosby's early unfettered strip humor and mobile line [174].

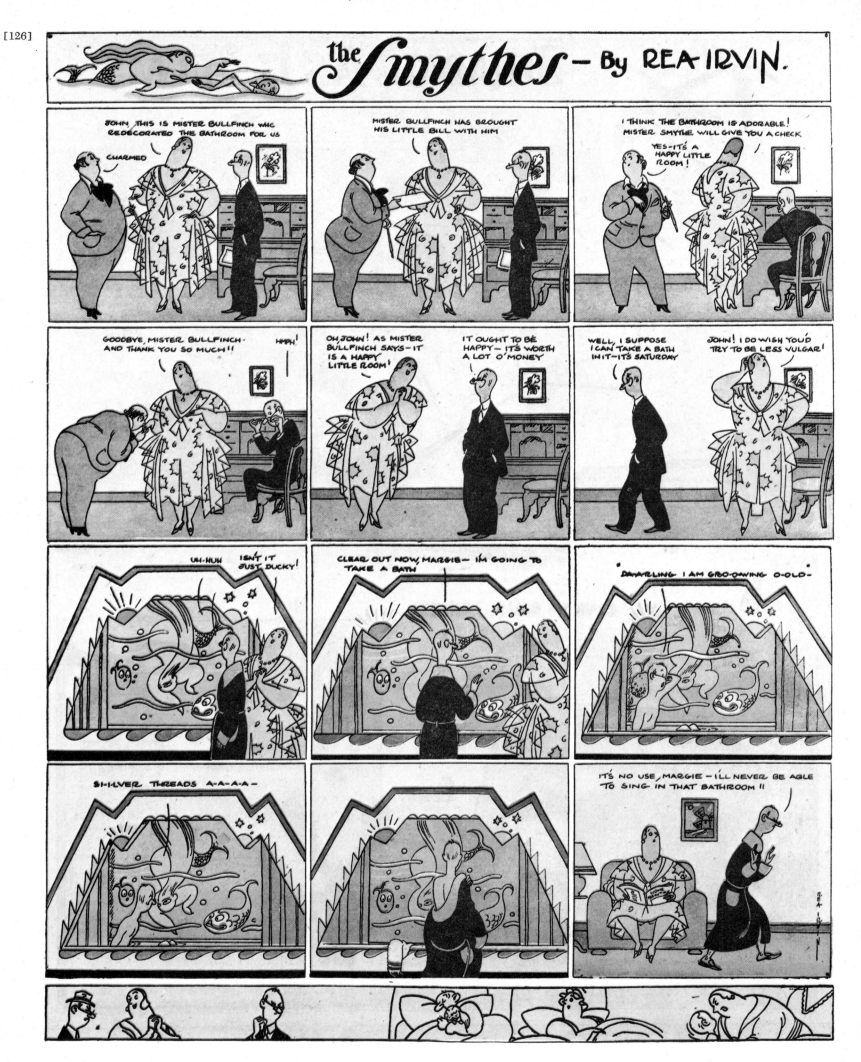

Polly and Her Pals

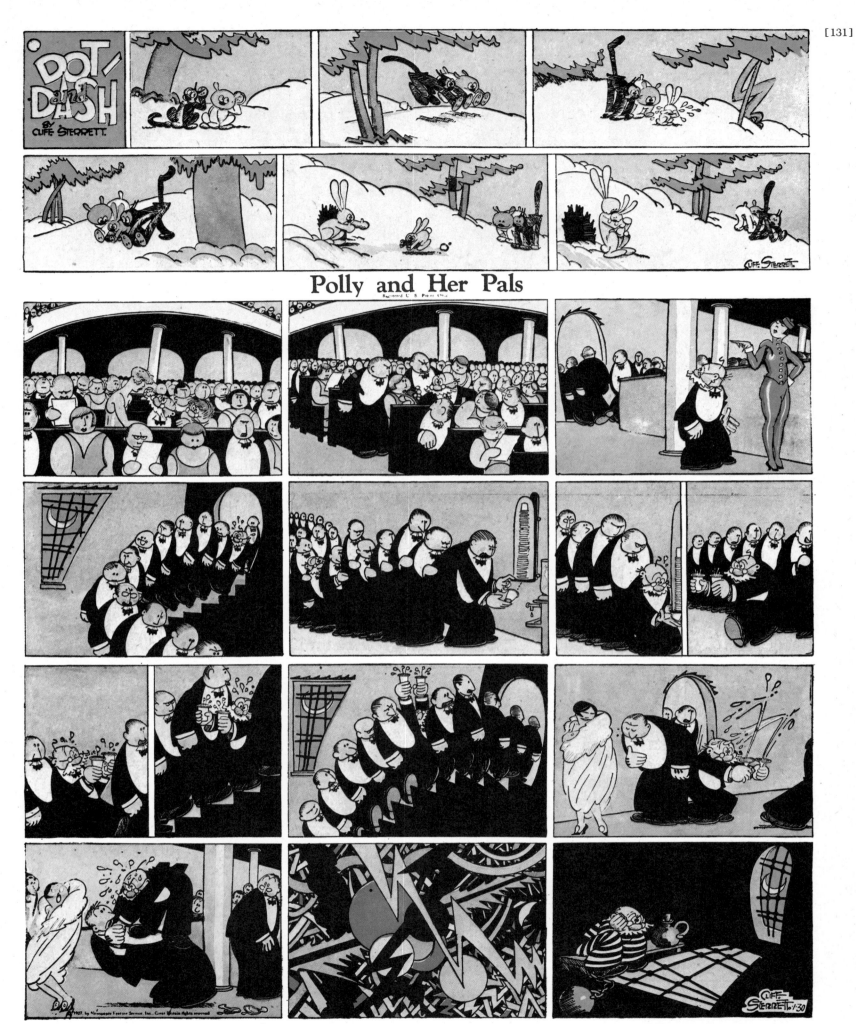

Polly and Her Pals

Polly and Her Pals

Polly and Her Pals
Registered U. S. Patent Office

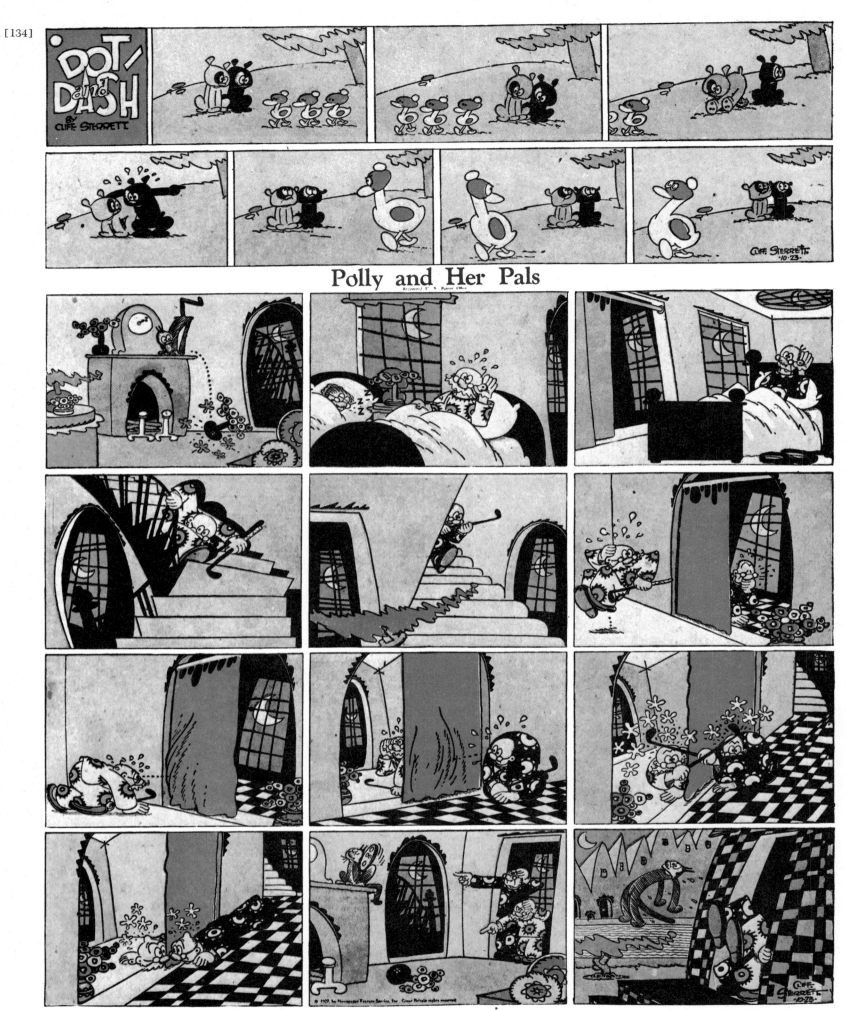

Polly and Her Pals

Polly and Her Pals

[136]

MUTT AND JEFF -:- They Fire Off Seventy-Five Pounds of Giant Powder -:- By BUD FISHER

MUTT AND JEFF   -:-   Mutt Needed a Blow-Out Patch   -:-   By BUD FISHER

95

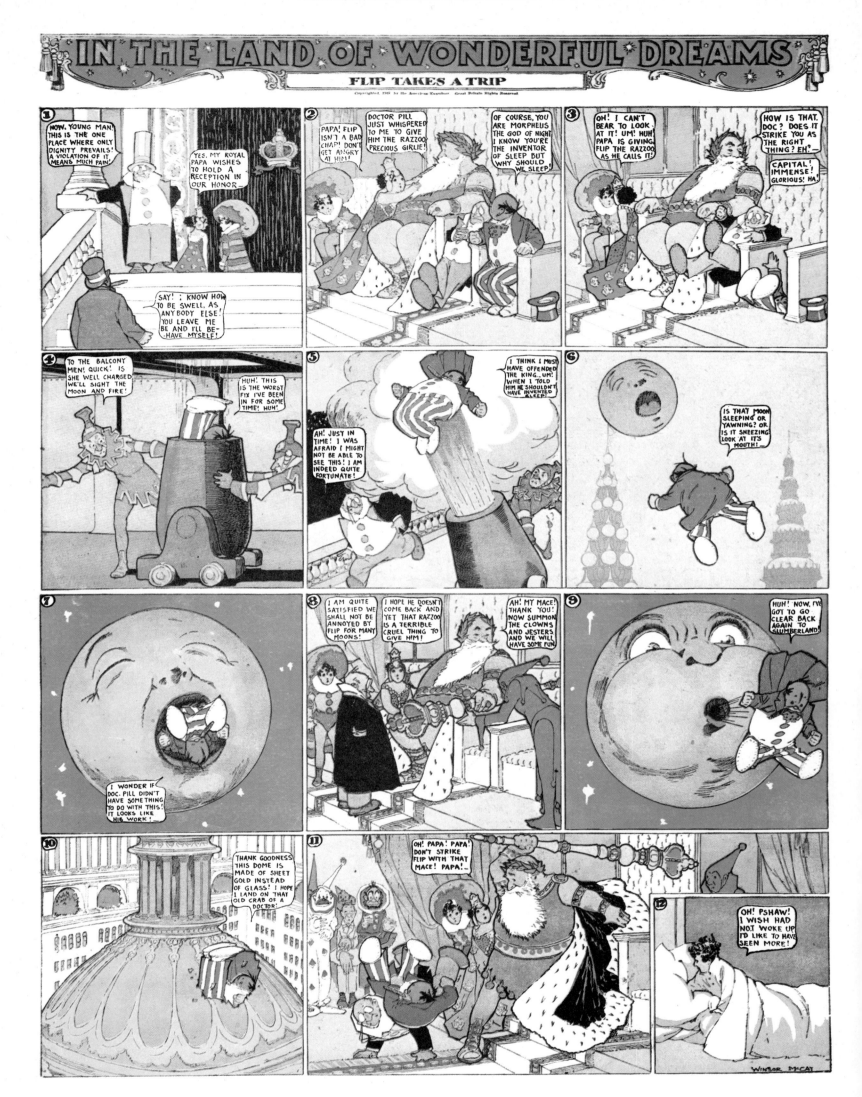

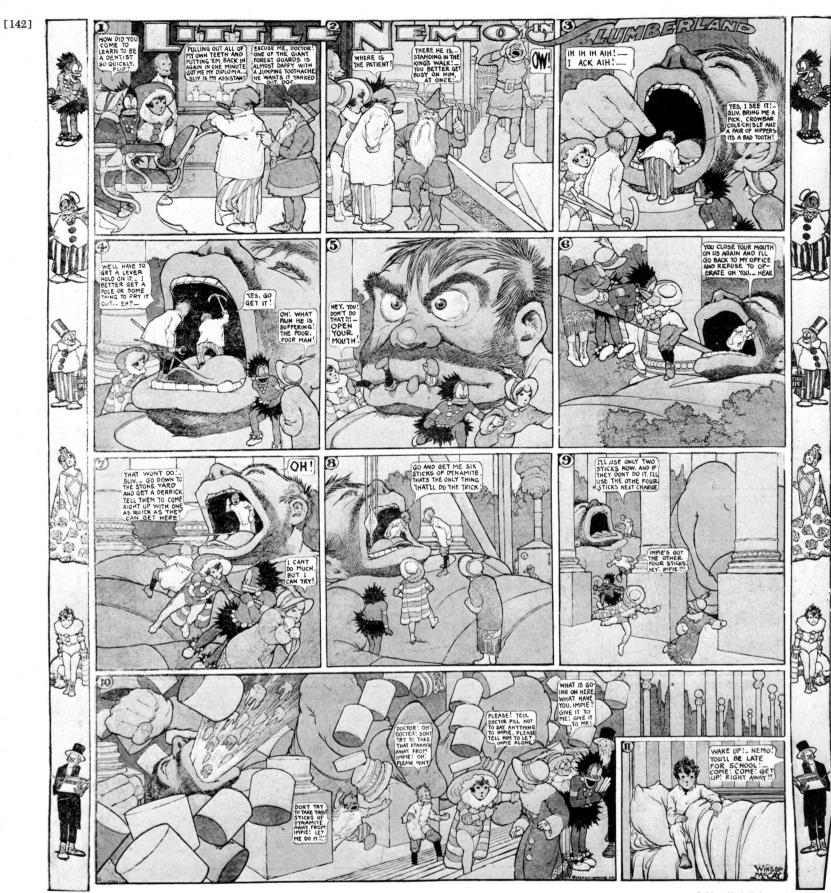

[144]

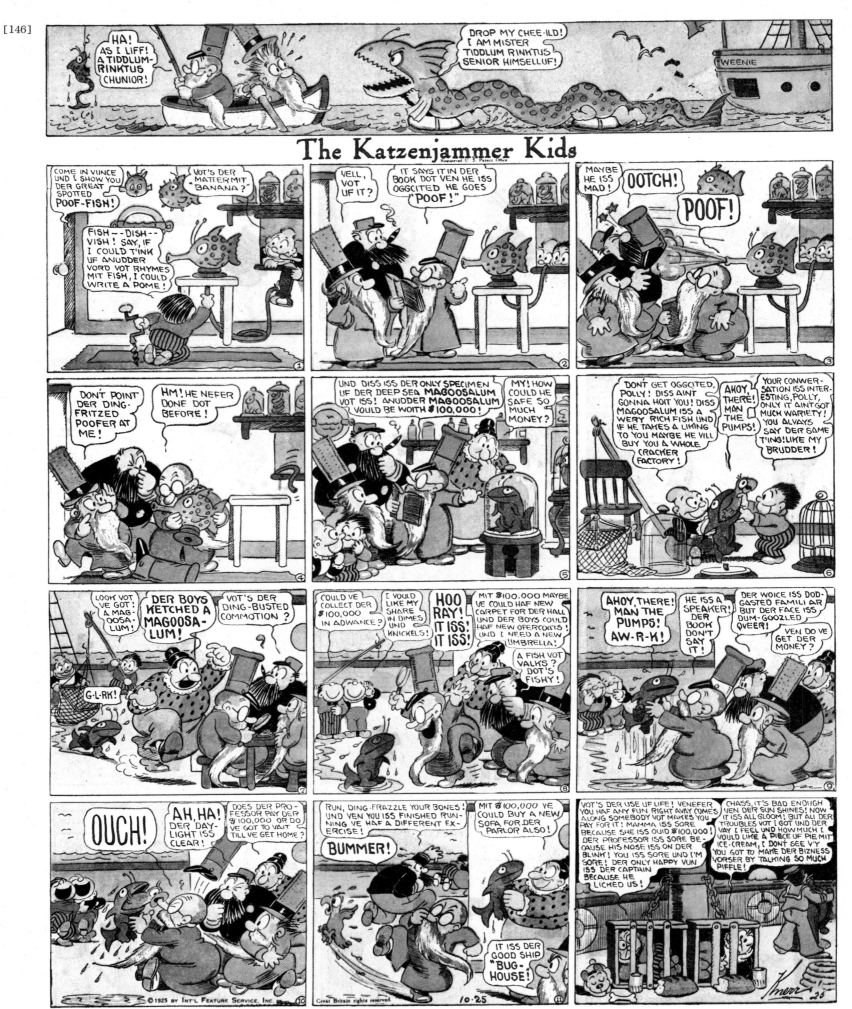

© International Feature Service, Inc., 1925

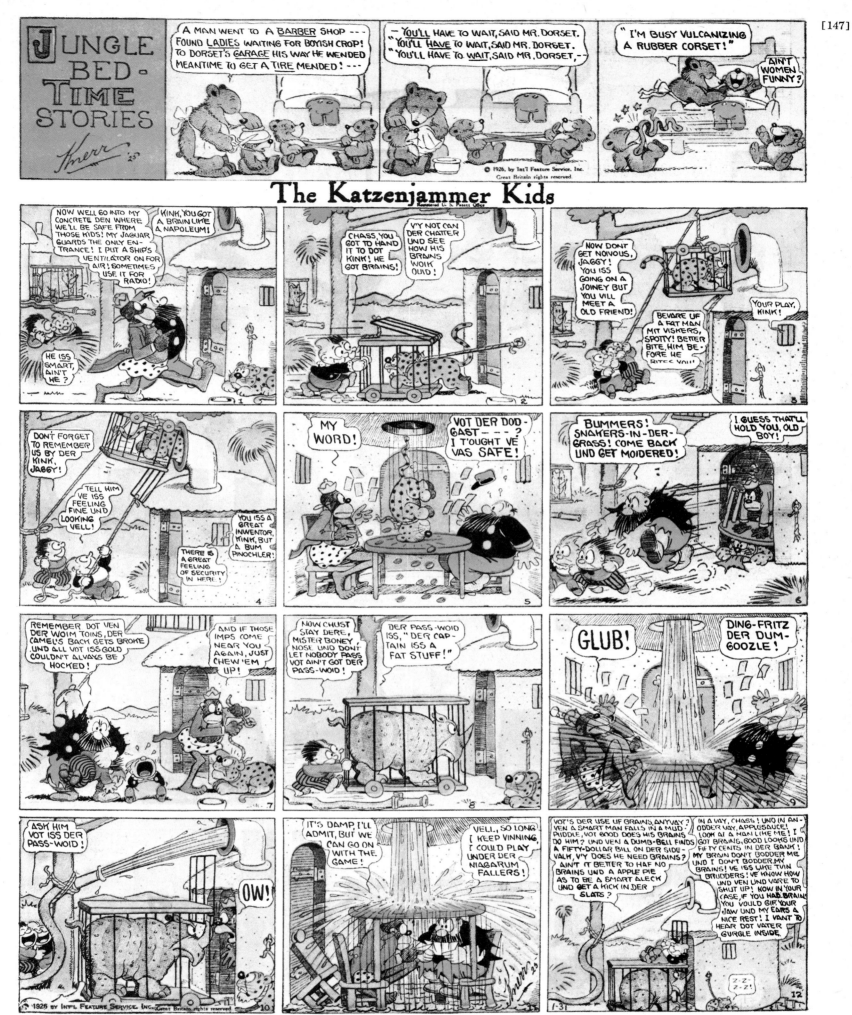

The Katzenjammer Kids

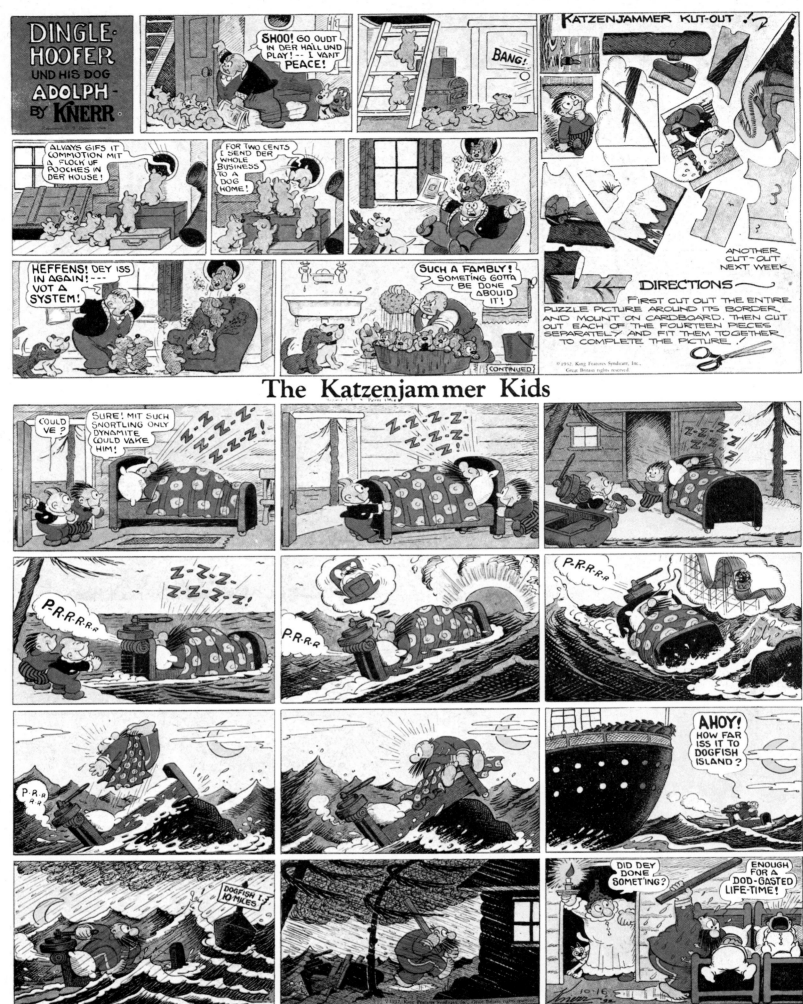

The Katzenjammer Kids

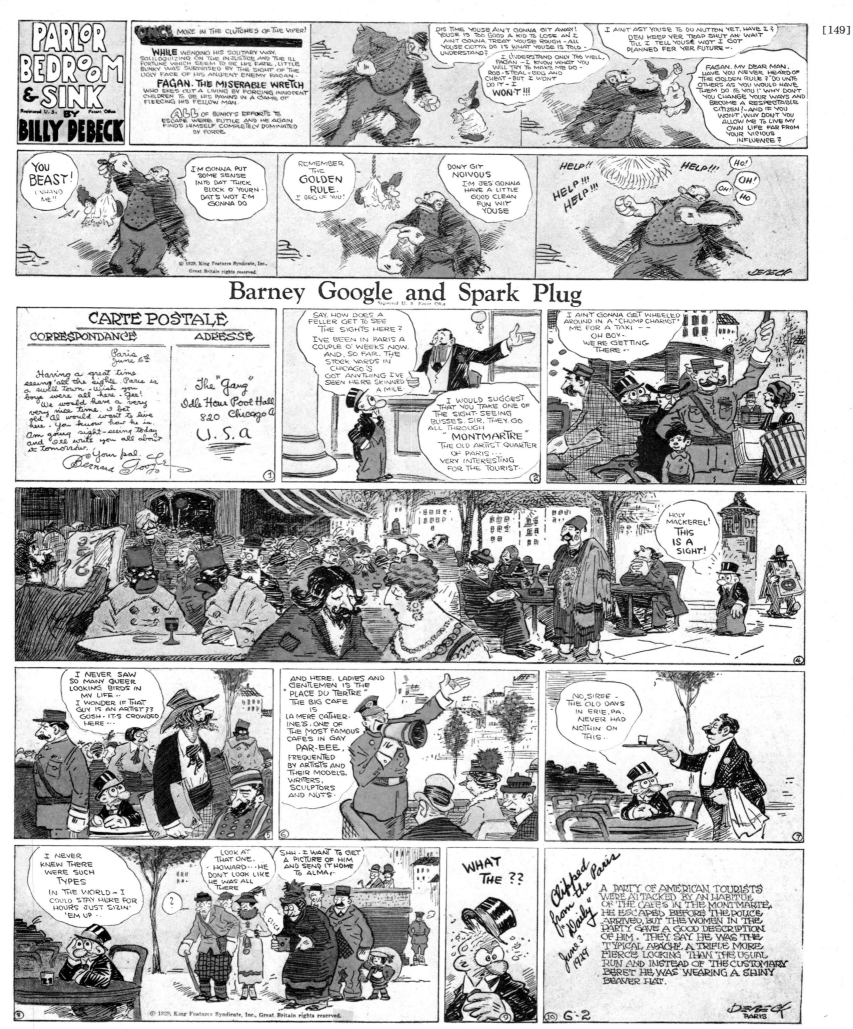

Barney Google and Spark Plug

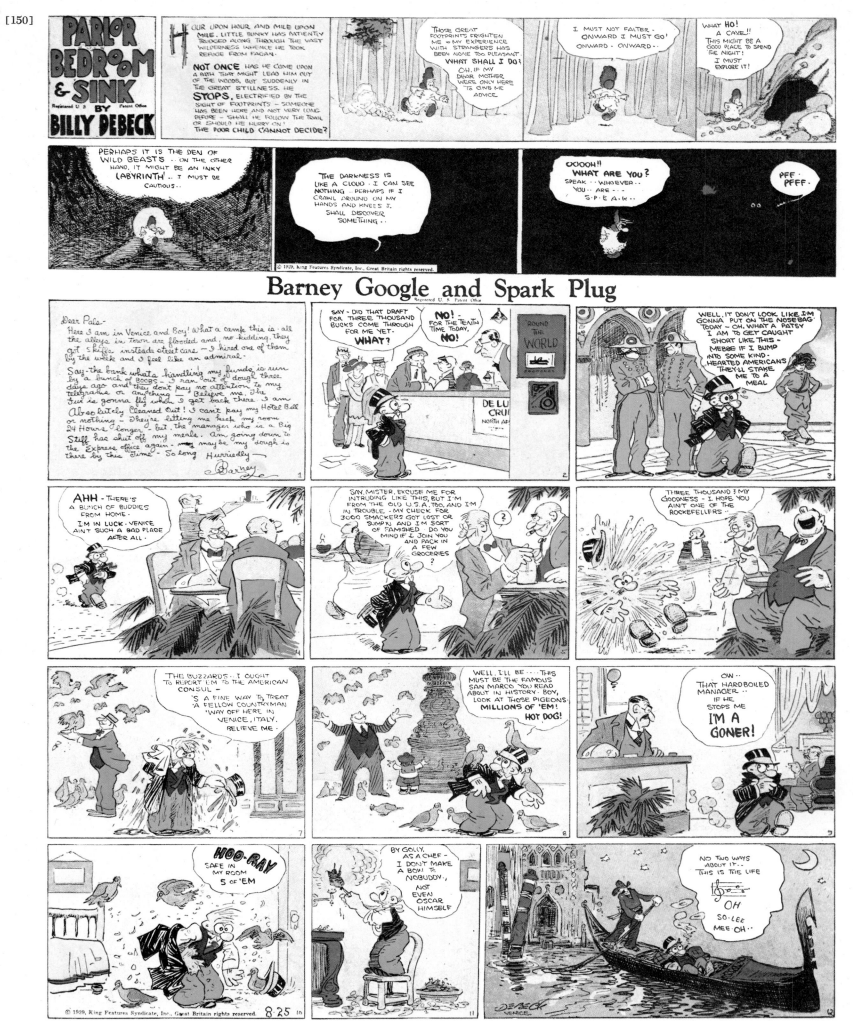

Barney Google and Spark Plug

© The Chicago Tribune, 1930

© The Chicago Tribune, 1930

THAT PHONEY NICKEL

THAT PHONEY NICKEL

THAT PHONEY NICKEL

Boob McNutt

COMIC SECTION OF THE
SAN FRANCISCO EXAMINER
April 18, 1920

Copyright, 1920, by Star Company.
Great Britain Rights Reserved. Registered U. S. Patent Office.

Boob McNutt

© Star Company, 1920

[162]

The Back-Seat Driver

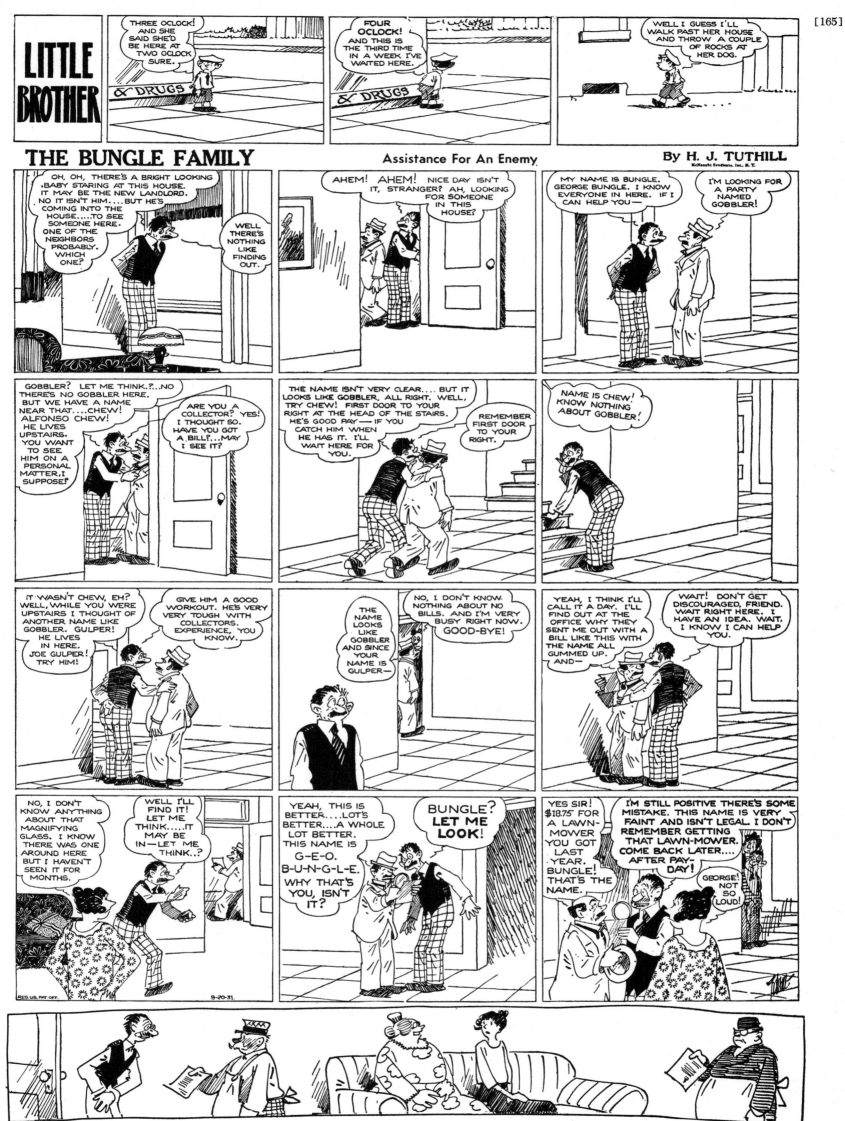

© McNaught Syndicate, Inc., N.Y., 1931

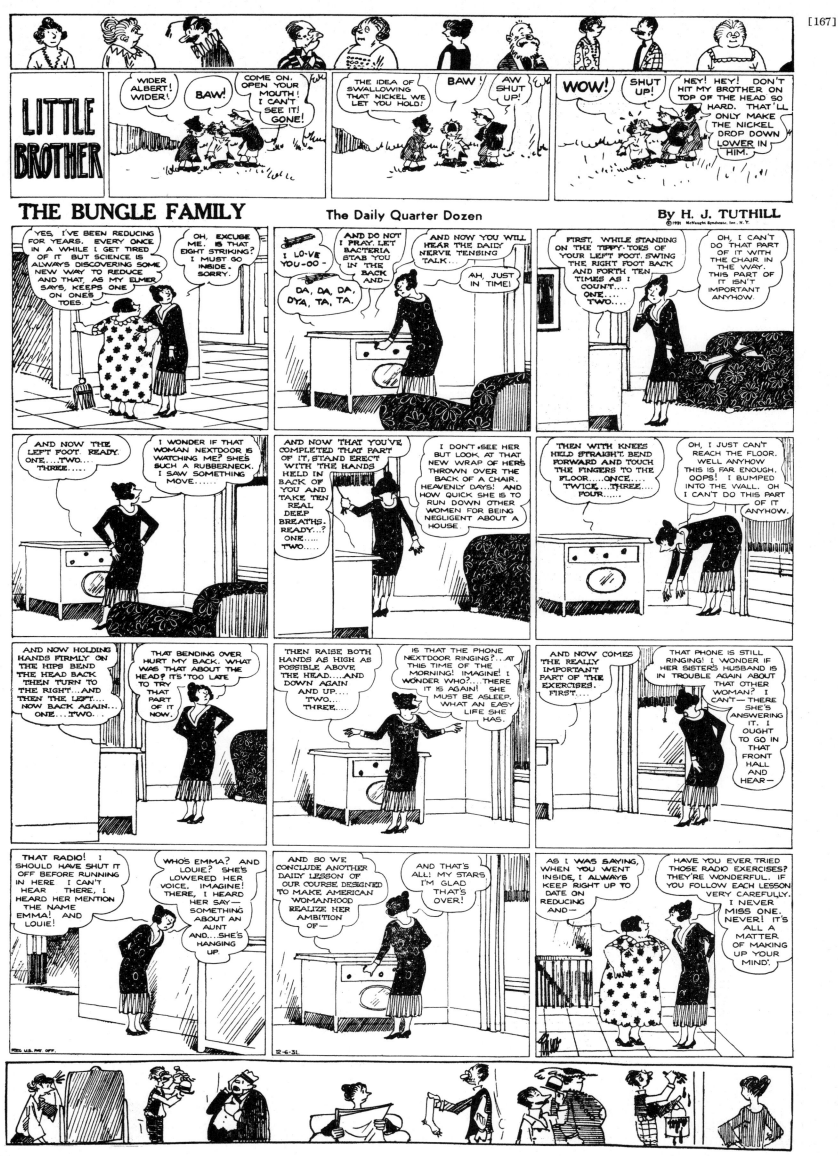

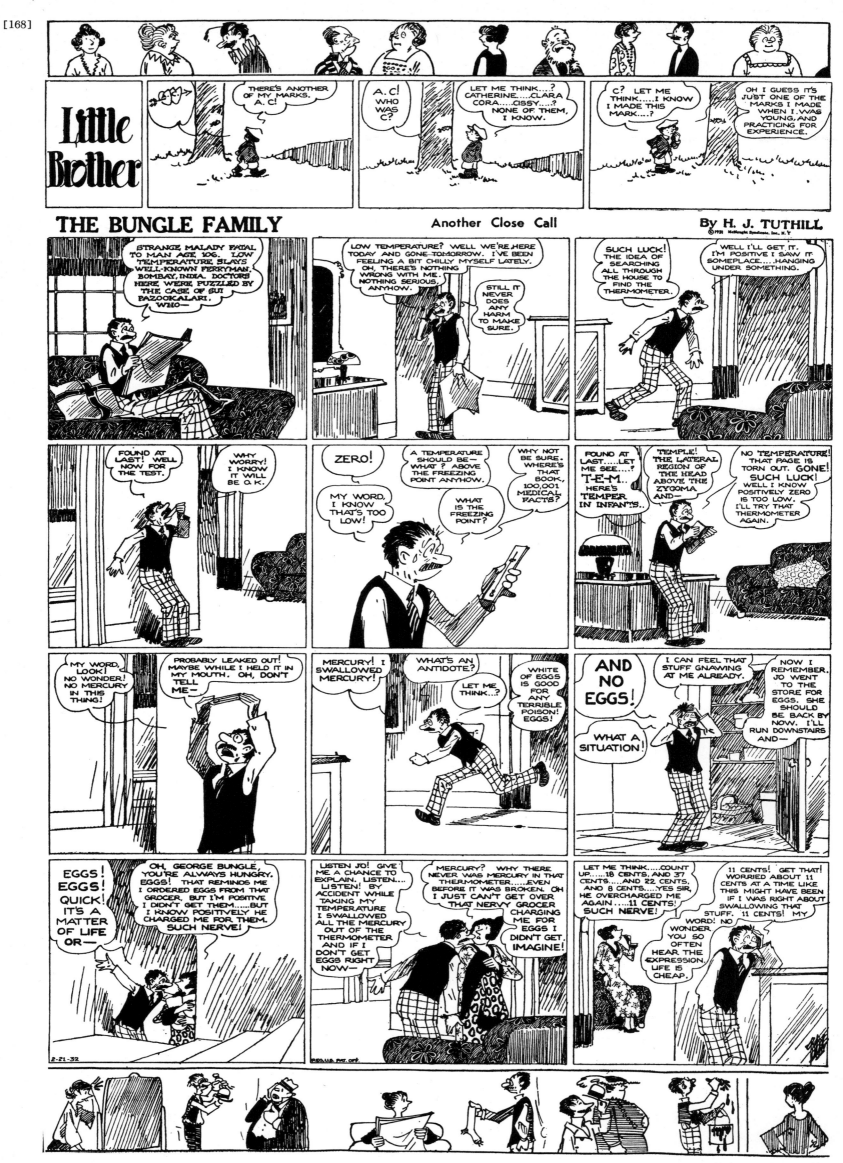

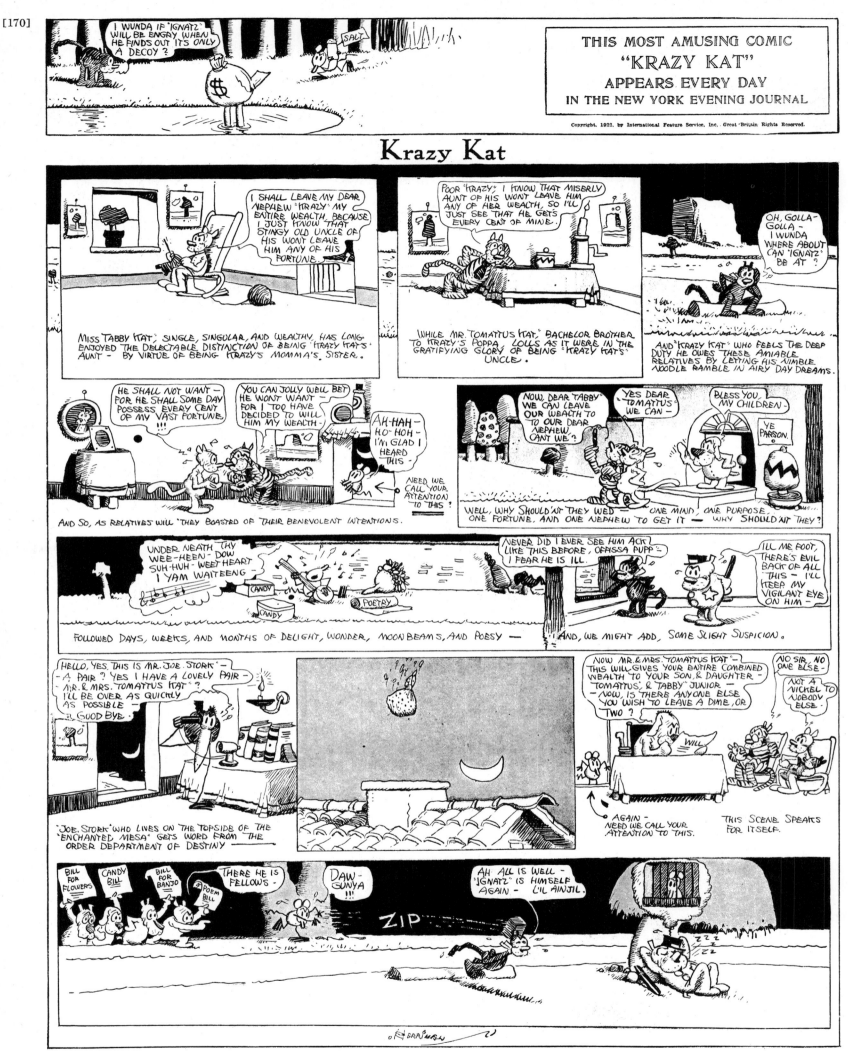

Krazy Kat

By Herriman

Krazy Kat - - - - - - - By Herriman

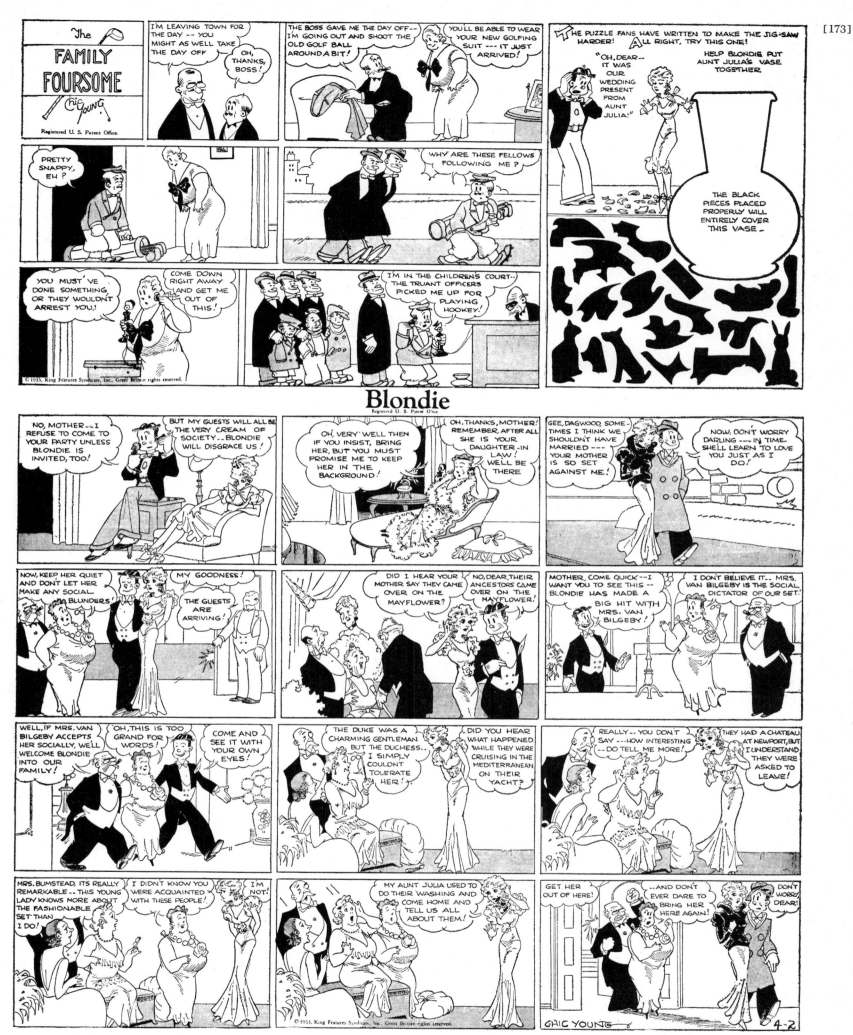

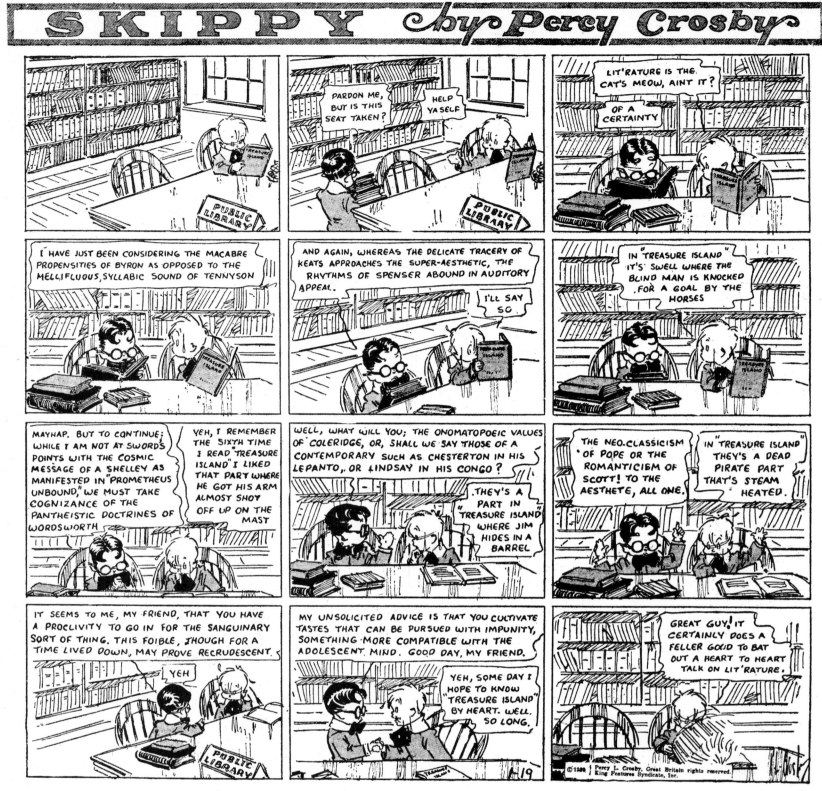

IV

Sunny Toonerville and the Darkling World

Anecdote and Narrative

in the Daily Comic Strip,

1917-1933

The reality of death, and the recurrent threat of it, on which adventure and detective fiction are based, came to the comic strip in the winter of 1925, quietly, unexpectedly, and somewhat obscurely. There had been hints earlier: a few men had been brought low as part of the plot mechanics in the movie satires of Ed Wheelan's *Minute Movies* and Chester Gould's *Fillum Fables,* but only as jests poked at the mayhem of some silent film melodramas. And a cold-blooded murder plot, which had been hatched against Oliver Warbucks in Harold Gray's *Orphan Annie* in mid-1925, built some brief suspense but ended farcically, with the plotters booted offstage. Roy Crane's *Wash Tubbs,* which had begun in early 1924 and was to become the greatest adventure strip of the 1920s, had not yet moved beyond comic melodrama and village romance, with an early seafaring treasure hunt handled largely as knockabout farce.

In *Phil Hardy,* however, a new, short-lived daily strip of late 1925, and in *Out Our Way,* an established daily panel anecdote strip with recurring characters and settings by J. R. Williams, a good deal of realistic blood was often shed in full view of the reader. *Out Our Way* was distributed largely to rural papers and second-string urban afternoon dailies, so that the impact of realistic death in the comics was somewhat muted. But the opening note for serious action and adventure had been struck, and the monopoly of humor on newsprint space began slowly but with an accelerating pace to yield to suspense and melodrama.

A few established strips moved to suspenseful adventure, notably Crane's *Wash Tubbs,* Gray's *Orphan Annie,* and Smith's Sunday *Gumps.* But most of the new emphasis came with new, largely daily, strips such as George Storm's *Bobby Thatcher* (1927), Gus Mager's *Oliver's Adventures* (1927), Hal Forrest's *Tailspin Tommy* (1928), Lyman Young's *Tim Tyler's Flying Luck* (1928), Monte Barrett's *Jane Arden* (1929), Rex Maxon's and Harold Foster's *Tarzan* (1929), and Phil Nowlan's and Dick Calkins's *Buck Rogers* (1929). After 1930 came the deluge, permanently altering the content of the comics pages with crime and adventure strips—*Skyroads, Jack Swift, Dick Tracy, Scorchy Smith, Dickie Dare, Patsy Ming Foo, Little Joe, Dan Dunn, Donnie, On The Wing, Broncho Bill, Brick Bradford,* and others, endless.

The major humorous strips held their own, retaining the static shape of yesterday and the day before, much as W. C. Fields and Laurel and Hardy brought their earlier comic trappings securely and successfully into the sound films of the thirties. The daily panels of *Toonerville Folks* and *School Days* illuminated the pages of the daily papers. *Moon Mullins* and *Minute Movies* continued to spin irreverent narrative of a high order. There were as many laughs as ever to be had. The comic strip had grown and performed an amoebic split into two spheres of appeal, but almost nothing was lost in the act, and a great deal was gained.

Notes on strips in this section

Out Our Way was a curious strip in that it alternated among as many as four separate anecdotal series, involving four separate sets of characters and settings, devoting one or two days per week to each continuity [175-178].

Moon Mullins and *Barney Google* were two of the great daily narrative strips of the 1920s and 1930s, as the selections included here will attest [221-319]. (Dover Books has republished two erratically condensed but still delightfully roguish Mullins narratives from 1929 and 1931 respectively.)

Another story strip of the period, which held readers for several decades, was Frank King's *Gasoline Alley*, but this work, extraordinary as it was in some ways as a chronicle of an American family, and unassuming as it was in its stance and tone, does not excerpt well: it depends heavily on the reader's intimate knowledge of what has happened before in the strip, and to whom. The same is true of the daily episodes of Sidney Smith's *The Gumps*, which were remarkable in that they gripped millions of readers with continuity on two disparate levels: that of a straightforward, bathetic, and deadly serious melodrama and that of a hilarious and deeply engaging takeoff on their own outward content. There is little doubt but that Smith, a Rabelaisian and irreverent man of comic wit and imagination, knew what he was doing to his readers on both levels, and as a greatly gifted storyteller was able simultaneously to satisfy the expectations of the two groups. But the story line is so complex and extensively developed that any excerpt of less than eight or nine months would fail to be self-explanatory as a unit. Regrettably, therefore, the daily *Gumps*, as well as the daily *Gasoline Alley*, have been passed over in this collection. Both surely deserve extended, carefully edited, anthologies.

Roy Crane's *Wash Tubbs* (published in a companion Sunday page as *Captain Easy*) is reputedly the finest adventure strip of its time, surpassed only after 1934 by the work of a man who had self-admittedly been Crane's devoted student: Milton Caniff and his *Terry and the Pirates*. The *Wash Tubbs* sequence reprinted here is regarded by its devotees as the graphic and narrative apogee of the strip [320-426].

Minute Movies   Edgar Wheelan   1929

© The Chicago Tribune, 1928

[229]

© The Chicago Tribune, 1928

[230]

© The Chicago Tribune, 1928

[231]

© The Chicago Tribune, 1928

[232]

© The Chicago Tribune, 1928

[233]

© The Chicago Tribune, 1928

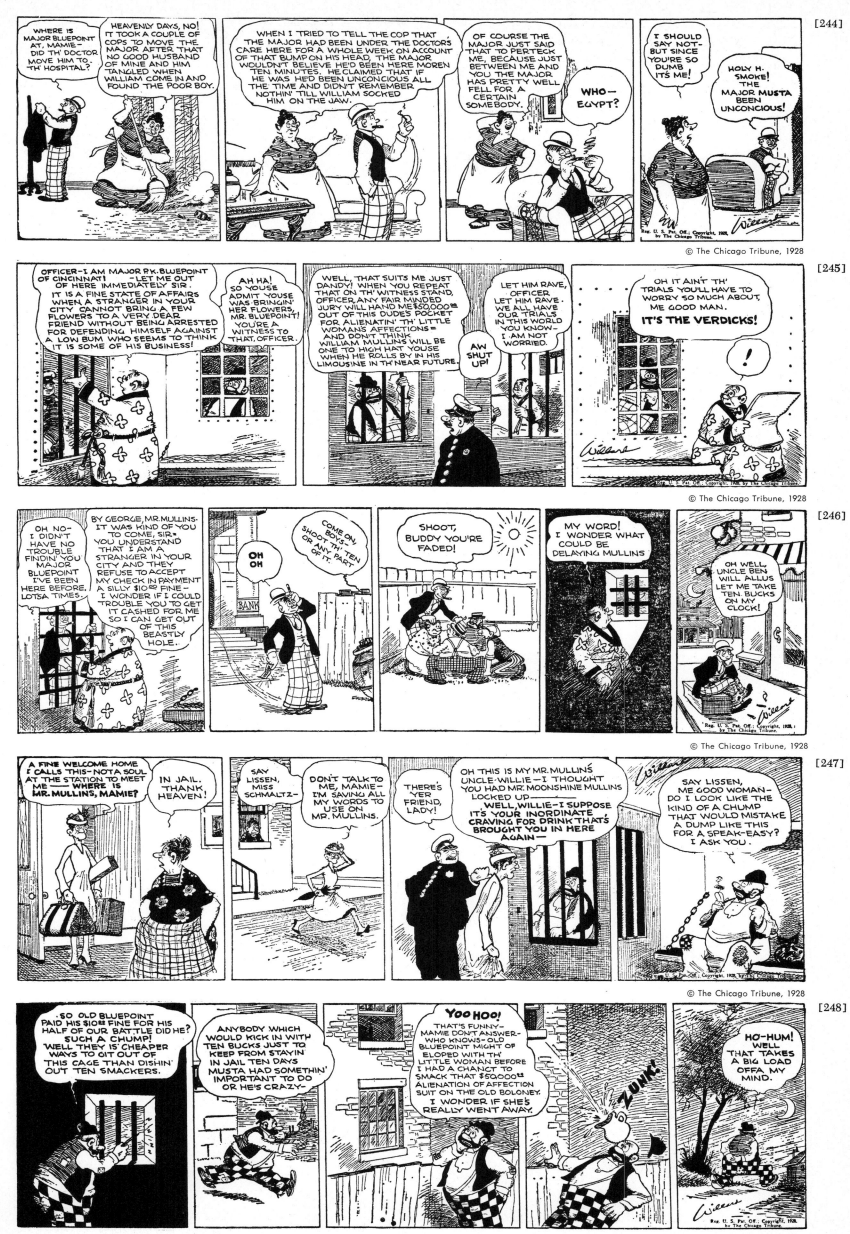

© The Chicago Tribune, 1928

© The Chicago Tribune, 1928

© The Chicago Tribune, 1928

© The Chicago Tribune, 1928

© The Chicago Tribune, 1928

[259]

© The Chicago Tribune, 1928

[260]

© The Chicago Tribune, 1928

[261]

© The Chicago Tribune, 1928

[262]

© The Chicago Tribune, 1928

[263]

© The Chicago Tribune, 1928

[269]

[270]

[271]

[272]

[273]

155

© King Features Syndicate, Inc., 1930

© King Features Syndicate, Inc., 1930

© King Features Syndicate, Inc., 1930

© King Features Syndicate, Inc., 1930

© King Features Syndicate, Inc., 1930

[288]

[289]

[290]

[291]

[292]

[293]

[294]

[295]

[296]

[297]

[313]

[314]

[315]

[316]

[317]

. . . The comic strip, especially after you leave the domestic-relations type which is itself realistic and unsentimental, is specifically more violent, more dishonest, more tricky and roguish, than America usually permits its serious arts to be. . . . Mutt and Jiggs and Abie the Agent, and Barney Google, and Eddie's Friends have so little respect for law, order, the rights of property, the sanctity of money, the romance of marriage, and all the other foundations of American life, that if they were put into (popular) fiction the Society for the Suppression of Everything would hale them incontinently to court and our morals would be saved again.

Gilbert Seldes
"The 'Vulgar' Comic Strip," The Seven Lively Arts, 1924

[337]

© NEA Service, Inc., 1933

[338]

© NEA Service, Inc., 1933

[339]

© NEA Service, Inc., 1933

[340]

© NEA Service, Inc., 1933

[341]

© NEA Service, Inc., 1933

[342]

© NEA Service, Inc., 1933

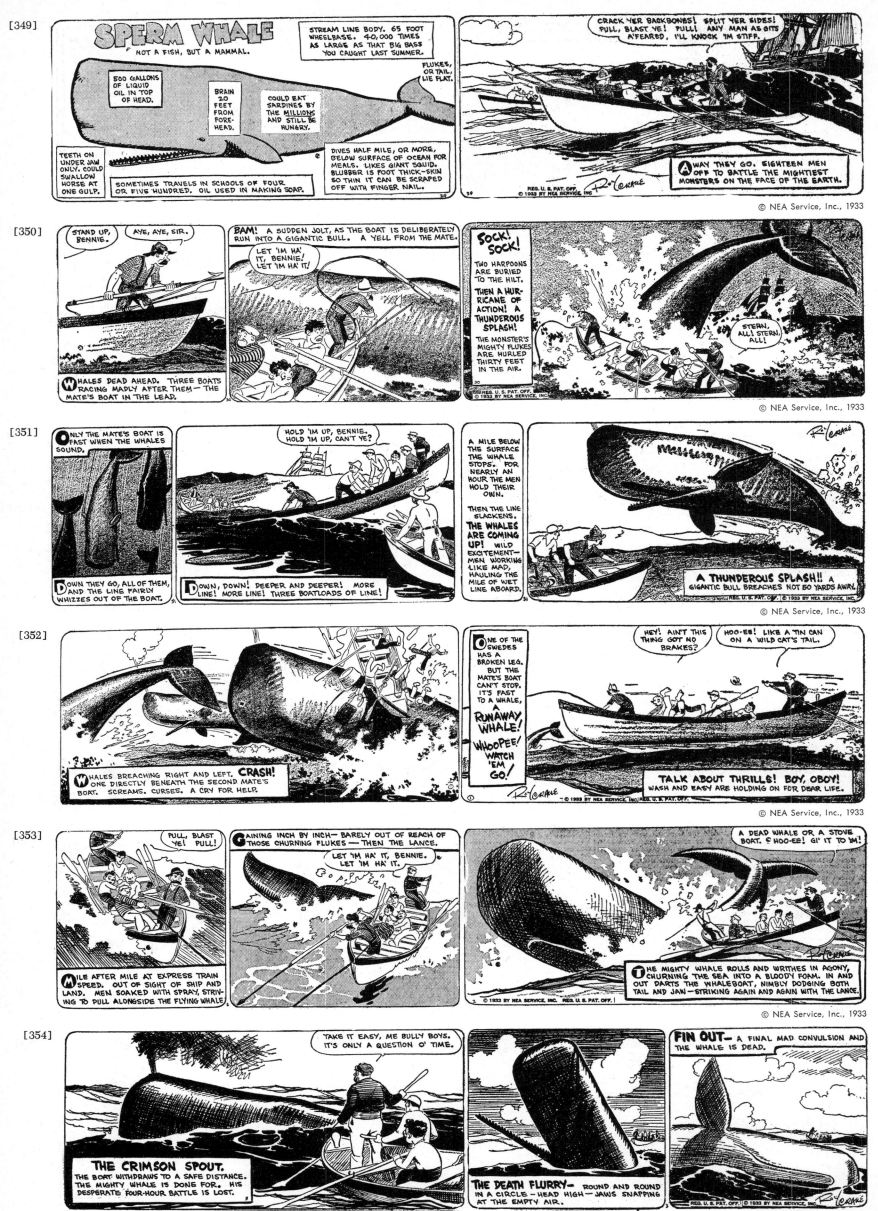

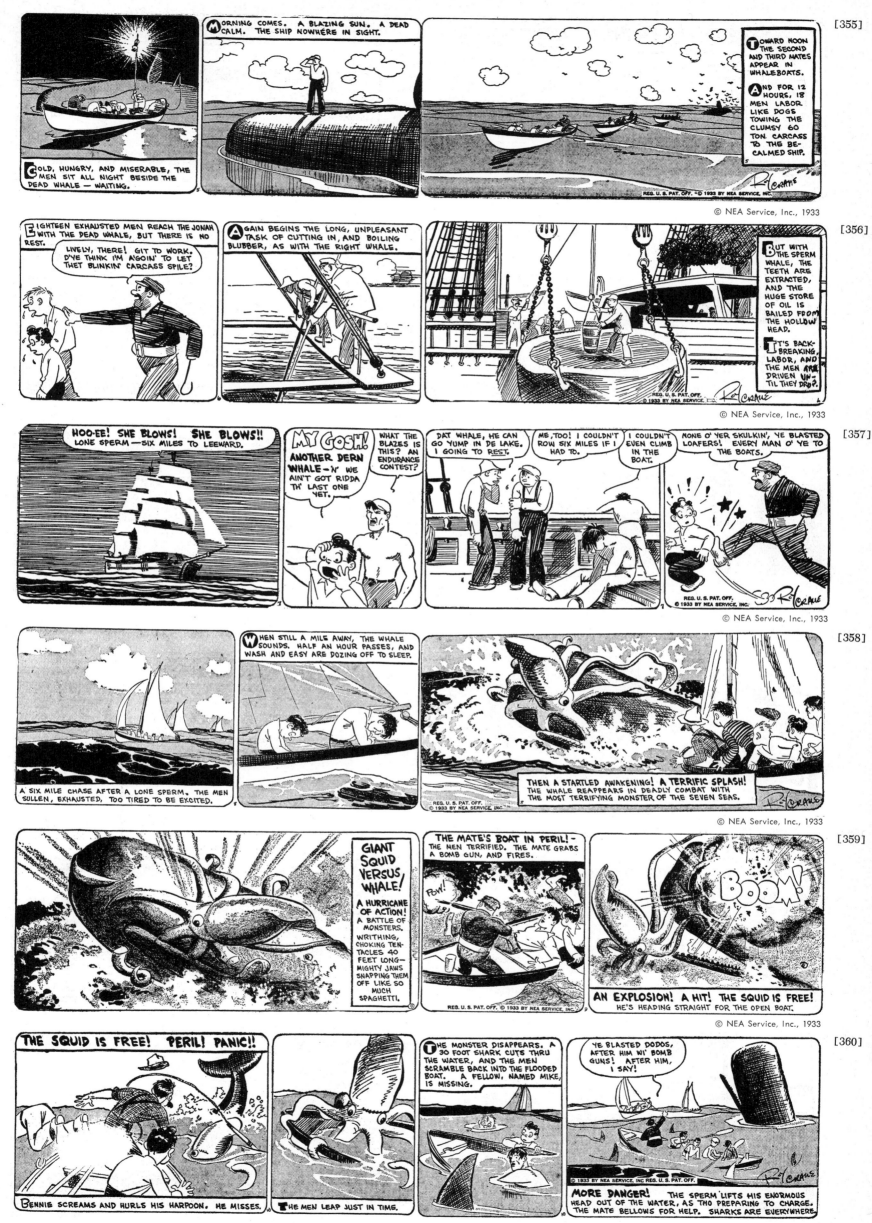

[373]

[374]

[375]

[376]

[377]

[378]

© NEA Service, Inc., 1933

© NEA Service, Inc., 1933

© NEA Service, Inc., 1933

© NEA Service, Inc., 1933

© NEA Service, Inc., 1933

© NEA Service, Inc., 1933

[379]

[380]

[381]

[382]

[383]

[384]

[397]

[398]

[399]

[400]

[401]

[402]

© NEA Service, Inc., 1933

[410]

[411]

[412]

[413]

[414]

[421] © NEA Service, Inc., 1933

[422] © NEA Service, Inc., 1933

[423] © NEA Service, Inc., 1933

[424] © NEA Service, Inc., 1933

[425] © NEA Service, Inc., 1933

[426] © NEA Service, Inc., 1933

Popeye, the Skipper, and the Abysses of Space and Time

Anecdote and Narrative in the

Sunday Comic Strip, 1930-1941

Adventure, crime, and comedy were as mixed in the Sunday comic pages after 1930 as they were in the daily strips, but a new narrative genre, science fiction, entered the serious comic strip at the turn of the decade. It had already been touched on humorously in such strips as Segar's *Thimble Theatre* and Kahles's *Hairbreadth Harry*. With the daily and Sunday *Buck Rogers,* the concept of time and space as a realistic, full-scale playground was transferred from contemporary pulp magazines into the comics, and almost immediately accepted by the public and by other comic-strip artists and writers.

An early close follower of *Buck Rogers* was the daily *Jack Swift* of Cliff Farrell and Hal Colson (1930). Another daily, *Brick Bradford,* by William Ritt and Clarence Gray (1933), followed a little later. And the celebrated *Flash Gordon* of Alex Raymond appeared in the Hearst Sunday pages in the first week of 1934. Science fiction themes also appeared on other and sometimes unlikely narrative strips such as Frank Godwin's *Connie,* Harry Tuthill's *The Bungle Family,* Chester Gould's *Dick Tracy,* Norman Marsh's *Dan Dunn,* Lyman Young's *Tim Tyler's Luck,* Lee Falk's *Mandrake the Magician* and *The Phantom,* and others. A most successful and well sustained comic treatment of science was in E. C. Segar's Sunday *Sappo,* where the brilliantly cracked Professor O. G. Wottasnozzle came up with continually ingenious and highly risible inventions.

The great old-timers in the strips continued as before, often untouched by the furor of action, adventure, and horror on the pages about them. McManus's Maggie and Jiggs went their bickering and battling way through the thirties as they had the twenties and teens before. The bucolic populace of Toonerville meandered as ever between the architectural bulk of Aunt Eppie Hogg and the mobile clatter of the Skipper's trolley.

New humor strips were introduced, such as Rube Goldberg's *Lala Palooza* and Ed Wheelan's *Big Top,* but there were few real successes in the thirties against the bizarre and exciting competition of the fantastic, criminal, and adventurous strips, although Lank Leonard's *Mickey Finn* and Al Capp's *Li'l Abner* survived the era handily, as did V. T. Hamlin's *Alley Oop.*

Notes on strips in this section

Dick Calkins drew only the daily *Buck Rogers*. Despite his signature on the Sunday pages of the early thirties, Russell Keaton was responsible for the striking artistry of the two pages which open this section [427-428].

The realistic or illustrative *beaux arts* style of drawings entered the comic strip with the advent of realistic adventure, although it was foreshadowed in the work of Winsor McCay. Probably its most effective use was in the work of Alex Raymond in his early (1934-36) *Flash Gordon* [430]; and in that of Harold Foster in his *Tarzan* period (1931-36) [429]. Foster's figures are often particularly notable for their movement and force. Almost universally published at the time in full-page size, with adequate space for the presentation of varying spatial concepts from panel to panel, the skillfully free-flowing and open style of both artists permitted the full integration of visually compulsive, multipanel movement and necessary narrative development so vital to the creation of effective comic-strip color pages.

Subsequent realistic work in the comic-strip vein, additionally hampered by the reduced reproductive space available in later years, has tended to be increasingly detailed, with an almost obsessive need to fill every part of every panel with black shadow and complex linework. Such visual weight can slow down a reader's eye movement across the narrative panels, and even draw his attention to irrelevant detail.

Like *Buck Rogers*, *Tarzan*, *Flash Gordon*, and *Prince Valiant* [431] are frequently reprinted here and abroad, and are (or soon will be) accessible to collectors in sizable editions.

One man who offered a highly fanciful Sunday page was V. T. Hamlin with his *Alley Oop* [432-434]. He was also the first major comic-strip artist to take the reader back into prehistoric time for his narrative setting, thereby reversing the direction of *Buck Rogers* and *Flash Gordon*.

With Cliff Sterrett, George Herriman, and Winsor McCay, Roy Crane was one of the great technical masters of the Sunday-page layout. In addition to his graphic dexterity with page space, Crane told a rattling, tongue-in-cheek adventure tale, which made his Sunday *Captain Easy* [435-437] the equal of his daily *Wash Tubbs* strip.

Little Joe [438-439], nominally bylined for Ed Leffingwell, Harold Gray's background artist for *Orphan Annie*, was in fact scripted by Gray through the thirties and early forties, and its characters were drawn by him for a number of years. This little-known Sunday half page was an entertaining and gripping strip. Replete with a sardonic and often bloody humor, *Little Joe* was a thoroughly adult strip. At the time it was relished by a few cognoscenti, but was apparently of little interest to the general public of the thirties, which still thought of western fiction in terms of Zane Grey, Richard Dix, and Tom Mix, and preferred western strip work of a similar nature.

White Boy [440-441] was another imaginative, nonderivative western strip of the time, drawn by *New Yorker* artist Garrett Price in an often stunning graphic style, and told by him with many skillful touches of the fantastic and unexpected. It was caviar to the average reader, had little circulation, and expired in the late thirties.

The extended *Thimble Theatre* Sunday sequence with which we close this section is not only the comic and narrative apogee of E. C. Segar's work, it may be the finest example of pure comic-strip narration [443-474]. Segar is almost unknown to any reader under fifty who has not encountered the only extensive reprint of his work since 1940 (the Nostalgia Press *Popeye the Sailor* collection of 1971). He based his humor on the interaction of one of the most inspired casts of comic characters this side of Dickens. (The inherent conceptual strength of many of his *Thimble Theatre* figures is perhaps demonstrated by their continued popularity in the hands of several successor writers and illustrators since Segar's early death in 1938.) But introductory words are unnecessary with Segar: the great sequence awaits only the turn of the reader's eye to the first episode to speak for itself in the salty, epic speech of Popeye, the propitiative murmur of J. Wellington Wimpy, or the cursing cackle of the Sea Hag.

© John F. Dille Co., 1933

SYNOPSIS—VAL APPEALS TO MERLIN, THE GREAT MAGICIAN, FOR AID IN RESCUING SIR GAWAIN FROM THE POWER OF MORGAN LE FEY, THE SORCERESS. MERLIN ASKS FOR SOME PERSONAL POSSESSION OF LE FEY'S WITH WHICH TO WORK HIS MAGIC AND VAL STEALS HER PET FALCON, BUT SO SWIFT IS THE PURSUIT THAT HE IS CORNERED AT MERLIN'S GATE.

SHOUTING LUSTILY FOR HELP, VAL HOLDS OFF THE ANGRY HUNTSMEN.

HELP COMES UNEXPECTEDLY.

MERLIN APPROVES OF VAL'S SOUVENIR.

MORGAN LE FEY IS FILLED WITH DREAD WHEN SHE HEARS WHO STOLE HER FALCON AND TO WHOM IT WAS TAKEN.

WISE MERLIN SETS TO WORK ON A MAGIC THAT WILL FORCE SIR GAWAIN'S RELEASE.

WHILE VAL WANDERS IN THE GREAT MAGICIAN'S ENCHANTED GARDEN.

BUT EVEN THE STRANGE ILLUSIONS THAT FILL THIS TWILIGHT PLACE CANNOT TURN HIS THOUGHTS FROM FAIR ILENE.

MIDNIGHT; AND INTO THE BEDCHAMBER OF LE FEY THERE COME CRAWLING STRANGE FANTASIES CONJURED UP FROM THE HALF-WORLD BY MERLIN.

NEXT WEEK—SIR GAWAIN IS FREED.

189

[432]

© New York News Syndicate Company, Inc., 1933

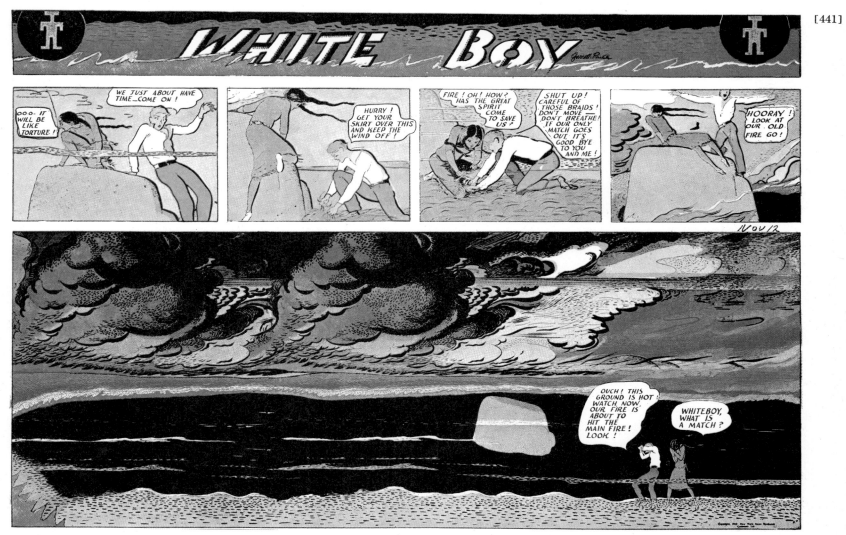

© New York News Syndicate Company, Inc., 1933

Thimble Theatre

201

Thimble Theatre

Thimble Theatre

Thimble Theatre

Thimble Theatre

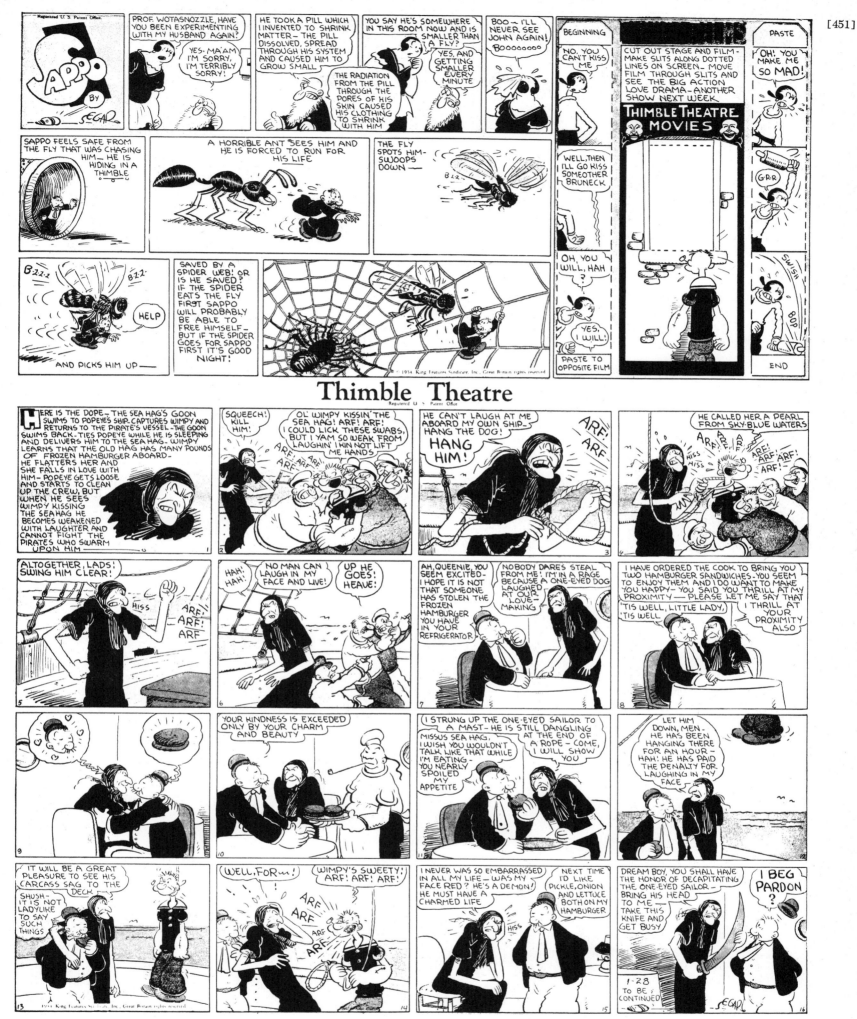

Thimble Theatre

Thimble Theatre

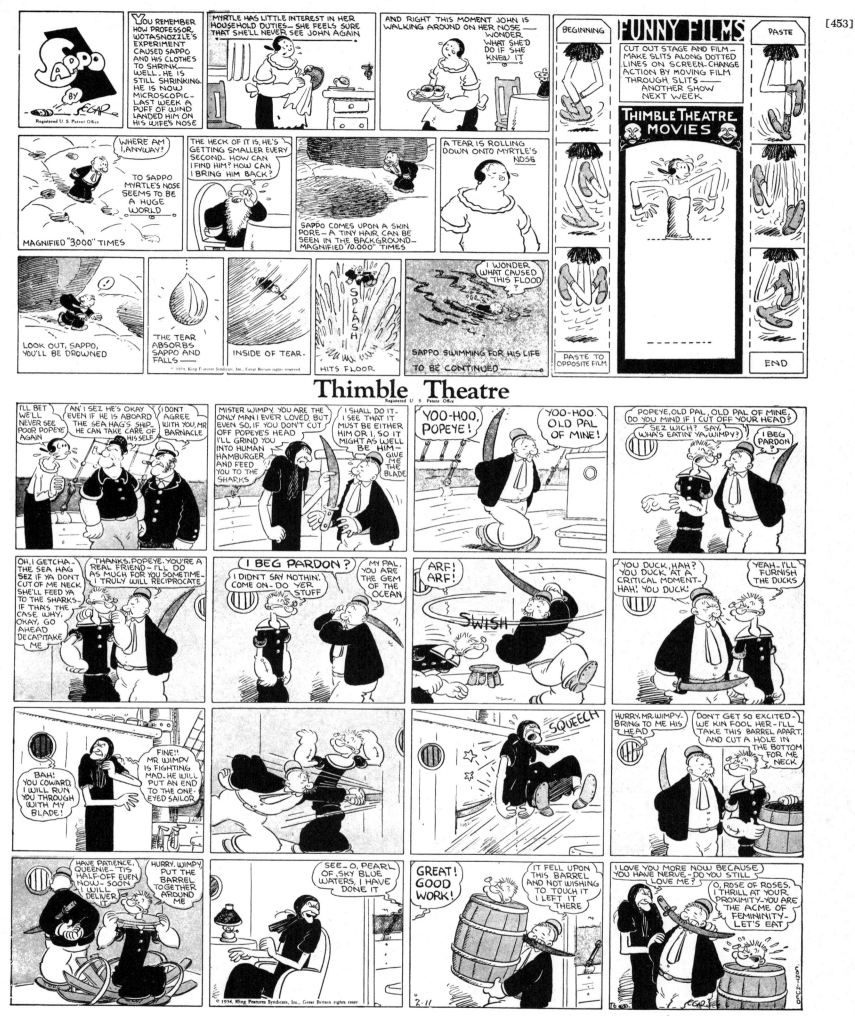

Thimble Theatre

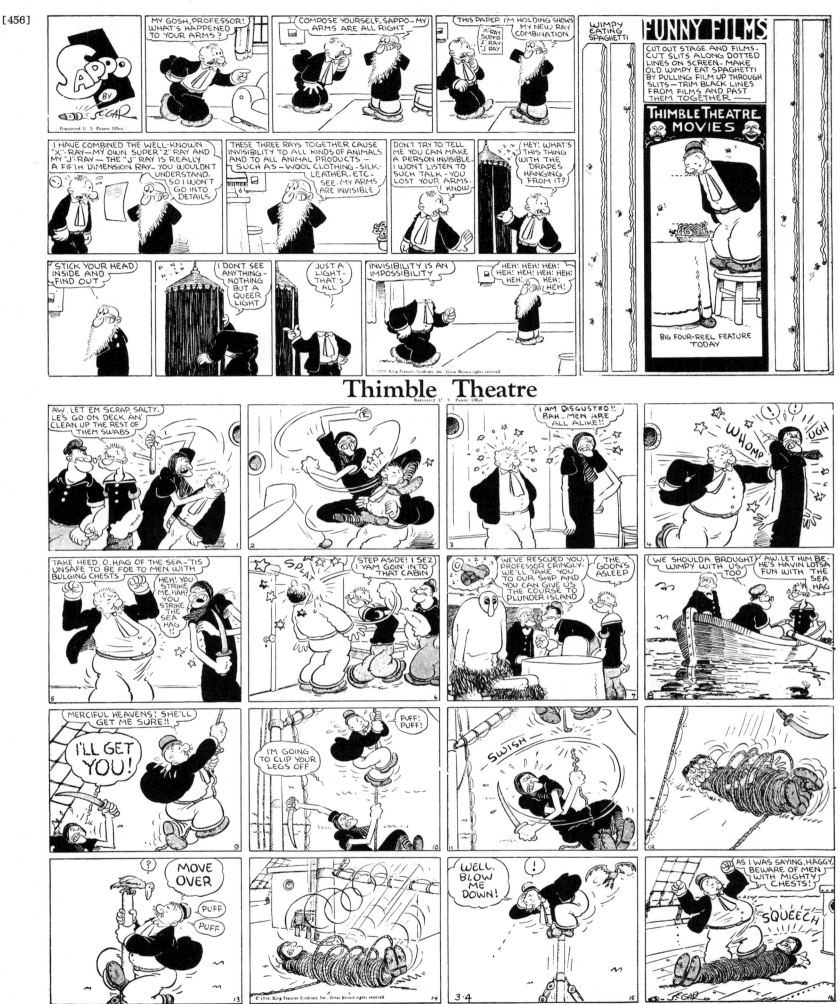

Thimble Theatre

Thimble Theatre

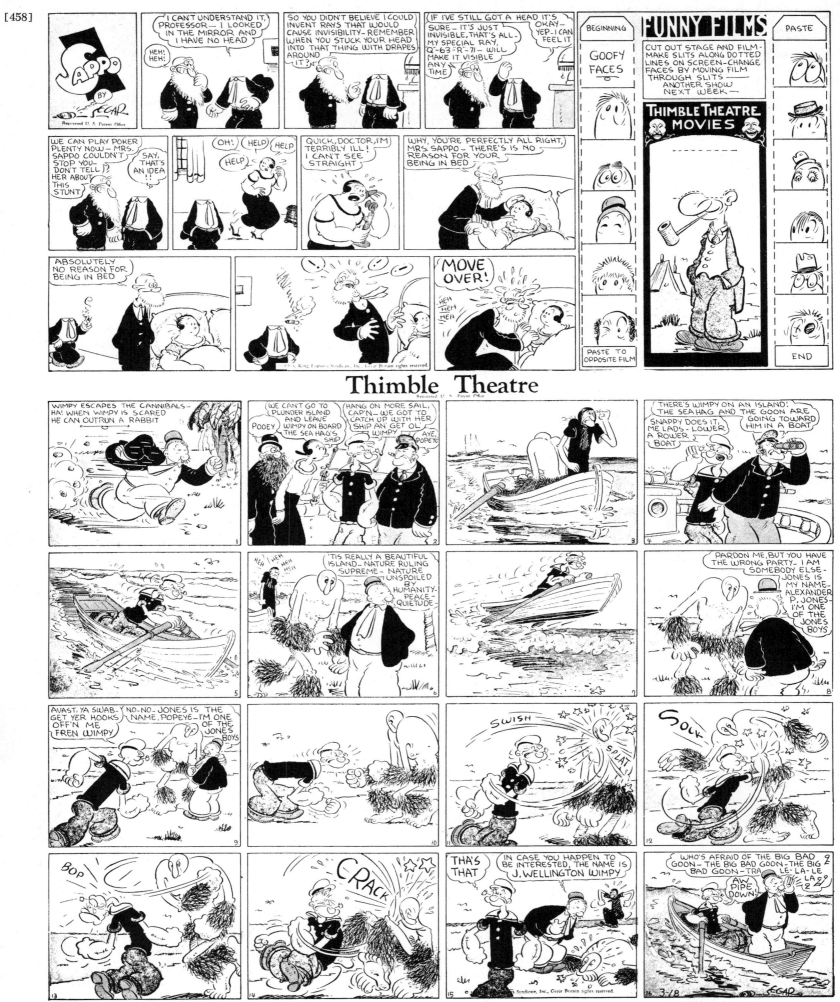

Thimble Theatre

Thimble Theatre

Thimble Theatre

Thimble Theatre

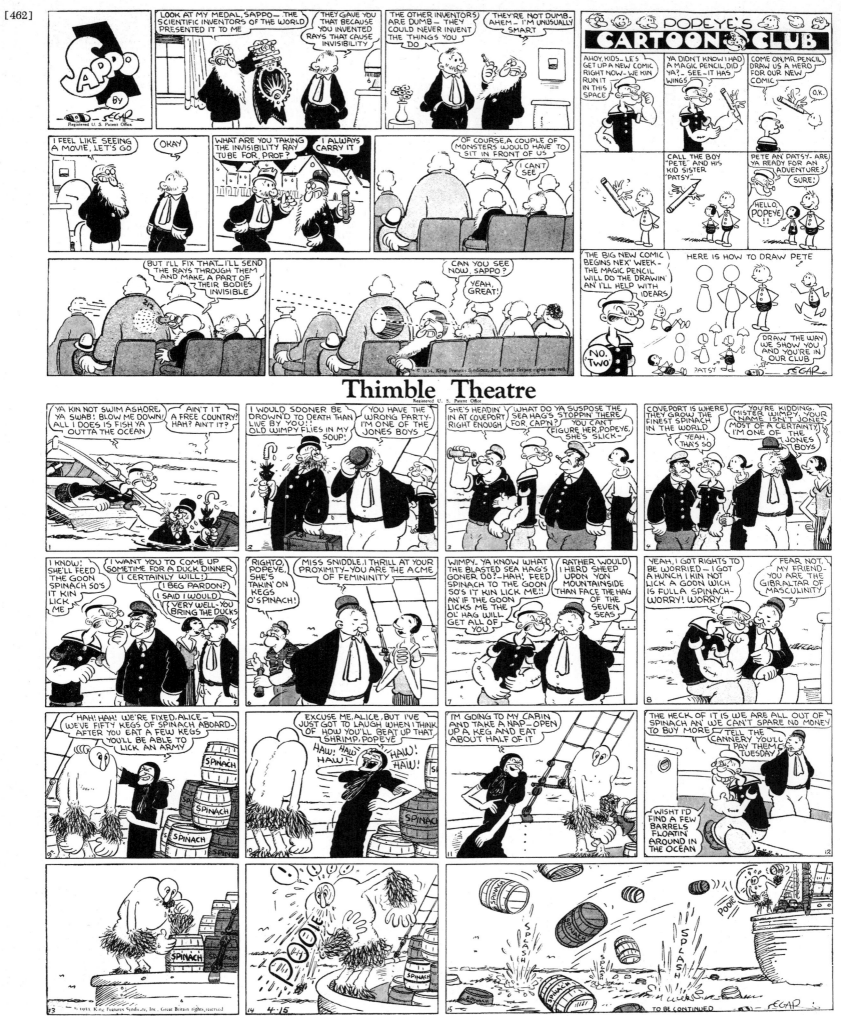

Thimble Theatre

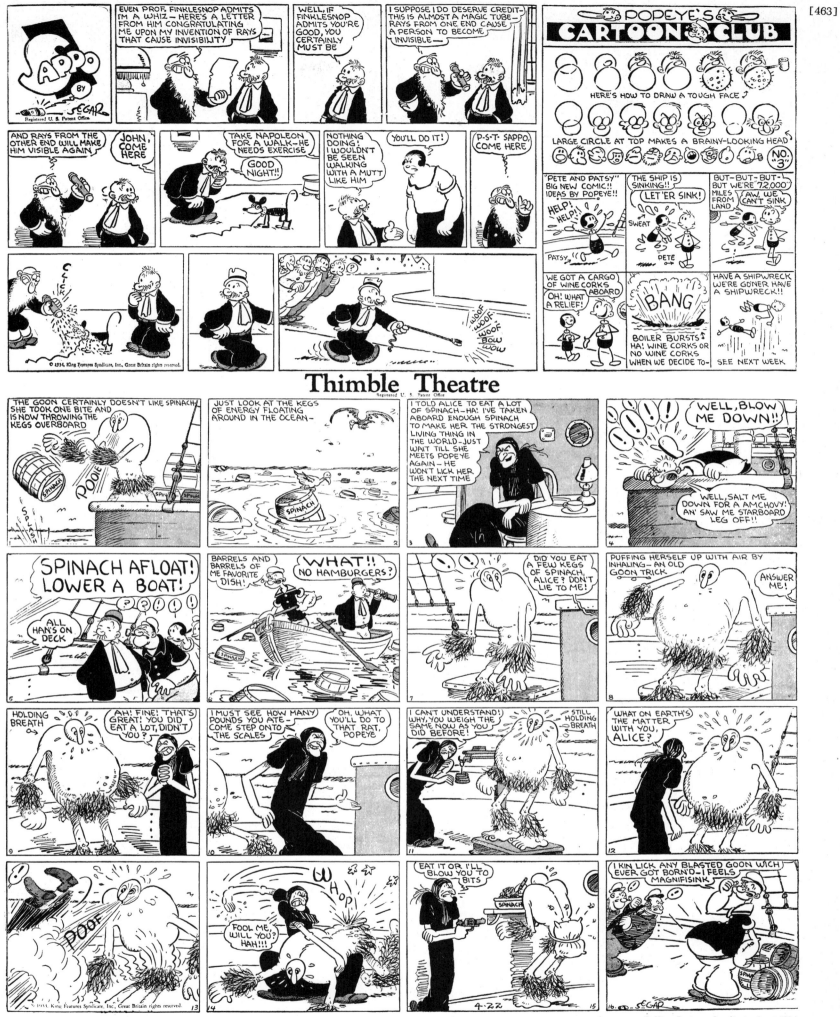

Thimble Theatre

Thimble Theatre

Thimble Theatre

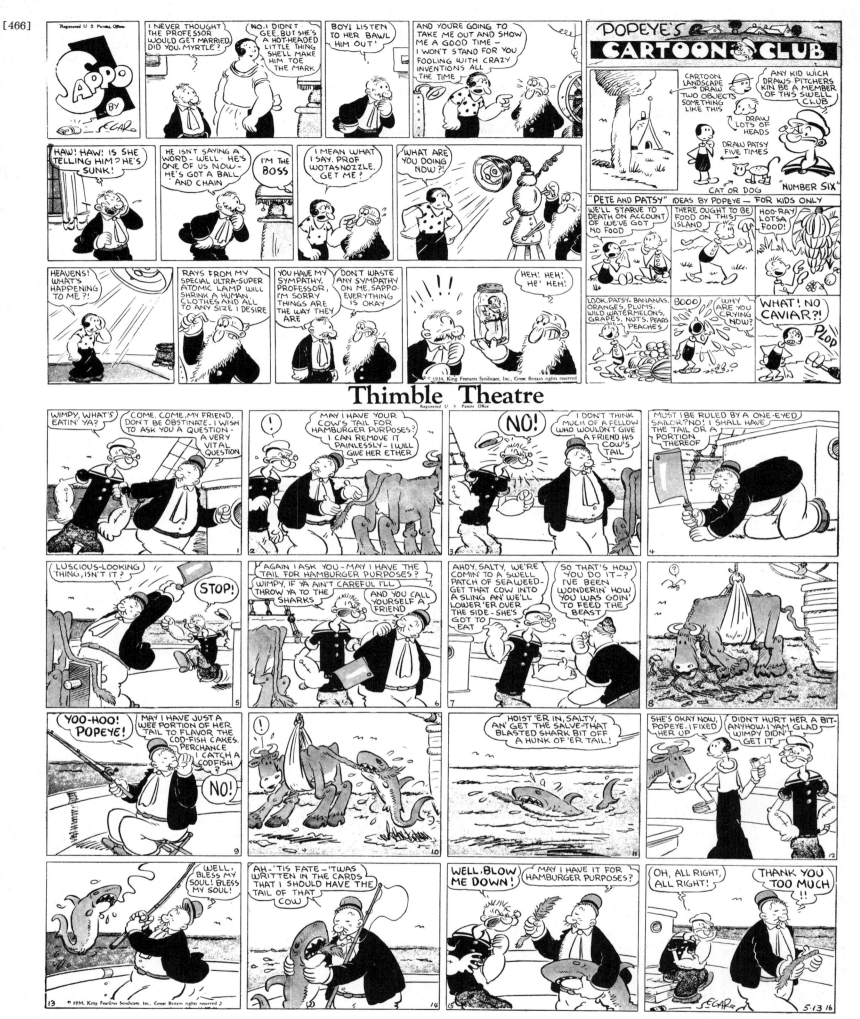

Thimble Theatre

Thimble Theatre

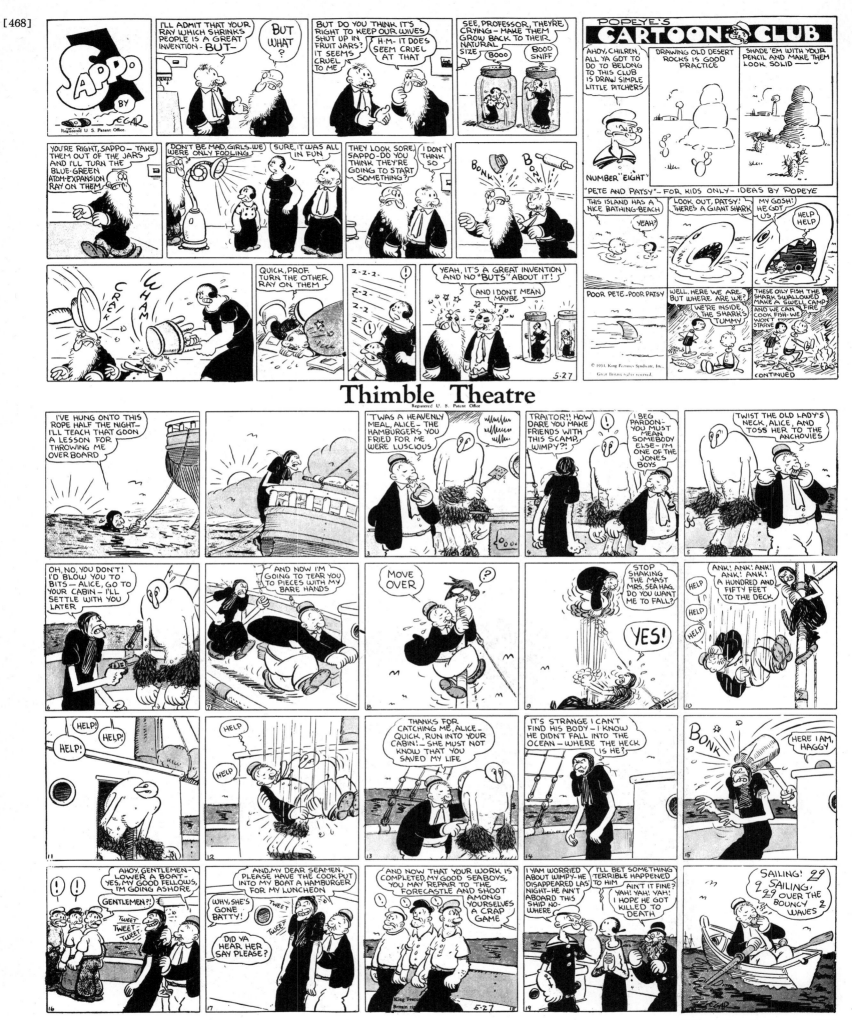

Thimble Theatre

Thimble Theatre

Thimble Theatre

Thimble Theatre

Thimble Theatre

Thimble Theatre

Thimble Theatre

VI

Shadow Shapes in Moving Rows

Extended Narrative in the Daily and Sunday Comic Strip, 1928-1943

There is little doubt that a day-to-day narrative continuity was attractive to the reading public in the comic strips of the thirties and forties. It was hard to find a simple anecdotal strip among the daily comics. Such strips as adhered to a daily gag pattern—Carl Anderson's *Henry*, or the Disney-produced *Donald Duck*, by Al Taliaferro, or J. Millar Watt's English import, *Pop*—stood out oddly among the multitude of story strips. Even the humorous strips from the twenties and before, such as *Bringing Up Father* and *The Captain and the Kids*, turned in the course of these two decades to story lines with carry-over subsidiary characters.

New daily narrative strips, with the most graphic pretension to realism, included Ritt's *Brick Bradford*; Falk's *The Phantom* and *Mandrake the Magician*; Briggs's daily version of *Flash Gordon*; Young's *Tim Tyler's Luck*; Forrest's *Tailspin Tommy*; Godwin's *Roy Powers, Eagle Scout*; Fanny Cory's *Babe Bunting*; Zane Grey's *King of the Royal Mounted* and *Tex Thorne*, with their various artists; and a number of others. Characterizations, plots, and dialogue tended to be stereotyped; the aim of the new narrative strips was at the audience for boys' adventure stories (although the leggy girls who paraded through *Mandrake, Flash Gordon*, and *The Phantom* probably drew some interested glances from adult readers too).

There was a good deal of genuinely inventive, sharply original, and often captivating narrative, serious and comic, among other daily strips of the period, and a number of examples have been selected for inclusion in this story-oriented section.

Notes on strips in this section — Alex Raymond's *Secret Agent X-9* of 1934-35, based in part on scripts by Dashiell Hammett, reads as freshly and forcefully today as it did at the time it was published. For a long period in the middle of 1934, when Hammett's script seems to have been adapted in unadulterated form by Raymond, *X-9* was so superbly executed and narrated that it seems one of the finest achievements of the story strip. The selection here [475-478] hints at the quality of the whole. Nostalgia Press has published much of *X-9* for 1934 and 1935 in one volume.

The *Abbie an' Slats* pages selected here incorporate the opening weeks of this beautifully drawn strip, for which Raeburn Van Buren maintained a high level of narrative and humor [485-496].

In *Barnaby,* illustrator Crockett Johnson brought a memorable whimsical fantasy (or *was* the fairy godfather fantasy?) to the comics pages, one which appealed to both adults and children. Our episode reflects its World War II-period origins [505-539]. (Dover Books has reprinted the *Barnaby* and *Barnaby and Mr. O'Malley* collections in current paperback.)

The *Mickey Mouse* narrative chosen here [542-643] is delightfully typical of those drawn by Floyd Gottfredson between 1930 and 1950. It is full of colorful incident and character and demonstrates the kind of absorbing, ingenious, risible comic-strip story often overlooked at the time by strip readers, who thought of the *Mouse* feature as intended solely to entertain children. The quality of these early *Mickey Mouse* narratives has recently been recognized by the Disney interests, and one, in a papercovered volume by Gold Key—*Mickey Mouse and the Bat Bandit*—has already been released.

With the last strip selections in this section, *Little Orphan Annie, Terry and the Pirates,* and *Dick Tracy,* we encounter the sequential linking of daily and Sunday strip episodes through continuous narrative, standard practice of the Chicago Tribune-New York Daily News Syndicate through which these three strips were distributed. These fine Tribune-News Syndicate strips have been widely reprinted in recent years in various formats. And *Little Orphan Annie* was reissued in the 1970s (with some minor but pervasive changes) in episodes that originated in the thirties. *Terry and the Pirates* is being reprinted from the beginning by Nostalgia Press and the first three volumes are available. Vintage *Dick Tracy* has recently appeared in a number of forms, including a paperback series from Fawcett Gold Medal Books.

The *Orphan Annie* selection included here may surprise many individuals who had assumed that the Harold Gray strip was an exercise in sentimentality and political conservatism. It was a work of a much higher order of narrative imagination than most strips. Gray devoted the majority of his waking hours to researching, writing, and drawing *Annie,* and he told an often gripping story with a variety of strong characters. This one, the end of a much longer narrative, is one of his best [644-672]. (Dover Books has republished two Annie narratives from 1926 and from 1933, as originally collected—and somewhat condensed—by the Cupples and Leon Company.)*

Most of the reprinting in recent years of Chester Gould's detective strip, *Dick Tracy,* has emphasized Gould's relatively fanciful work of the forties, with its amusing galaxy of grotesque villains (Flattop, Pruneface, and the rest). Here we draw on his often savagely realistic material of the middle thirties, the pursuit and dispatching of Boris Arson. Gould's delineation of the character and the environment of a type of midwestern desperado of the period (for example, Cutie Diamond) is exceptional, as is his handling of the Indian officer working with Tracy, unusual and interesting in the context of the time [688-715].

* Hardcover anthologies which draw on *Little Orphan Annie* (daily episodes only), *Dick Tracy* (again dailies only), *Toonerville Folks, The Gumps, Bringing Up Father,* and *Buck Rogers* have appeared recently enough still to be found in "remainder" bookshops and on bargain tables.

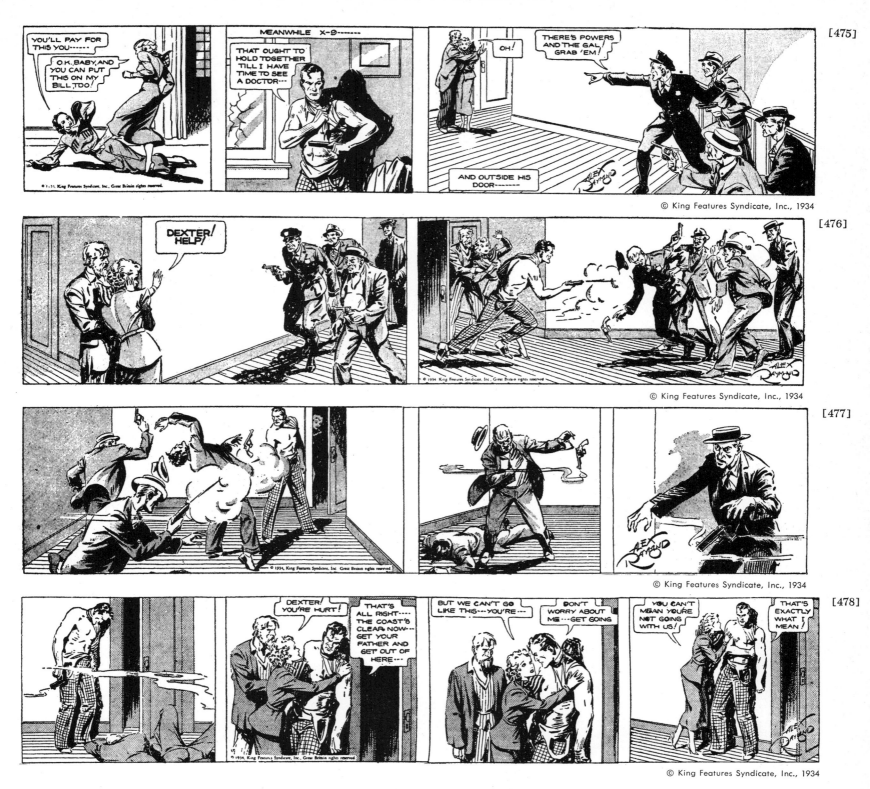

Bringing Up Father   George McManus   1936

Our Boarding House   Gene Ahern   1929

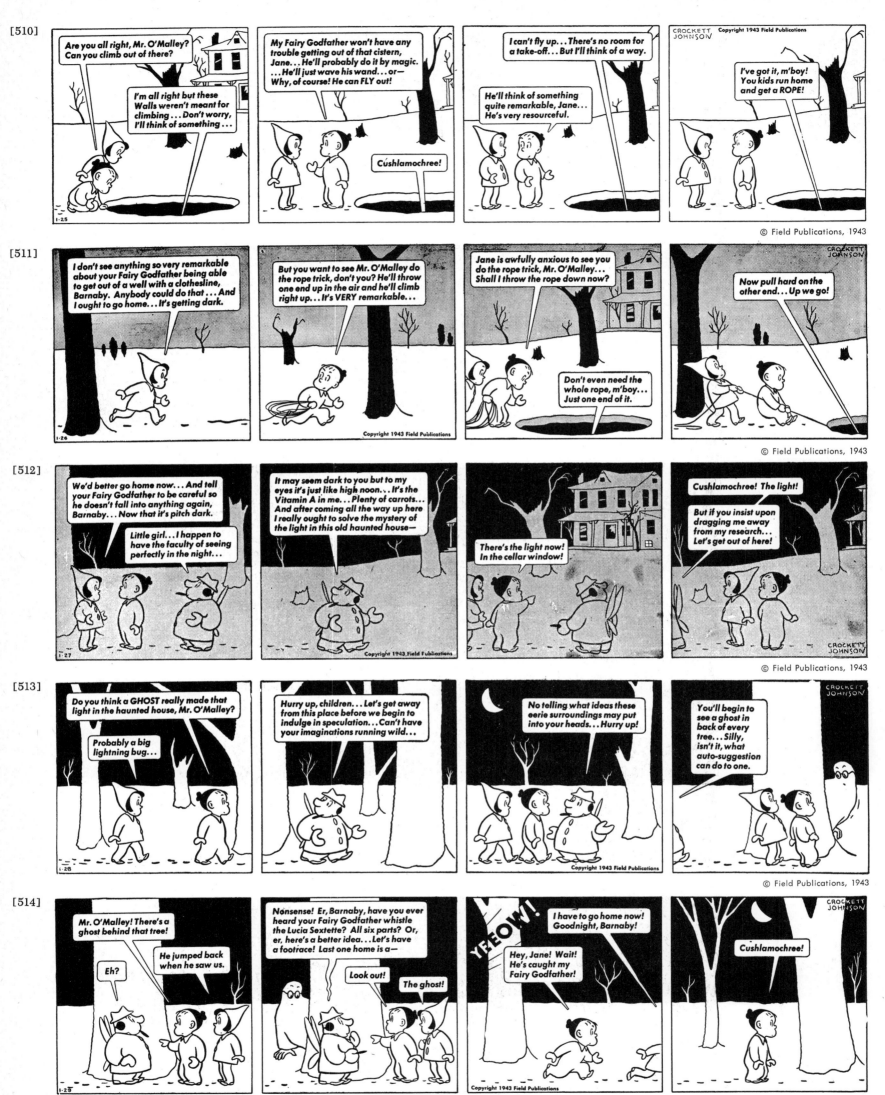

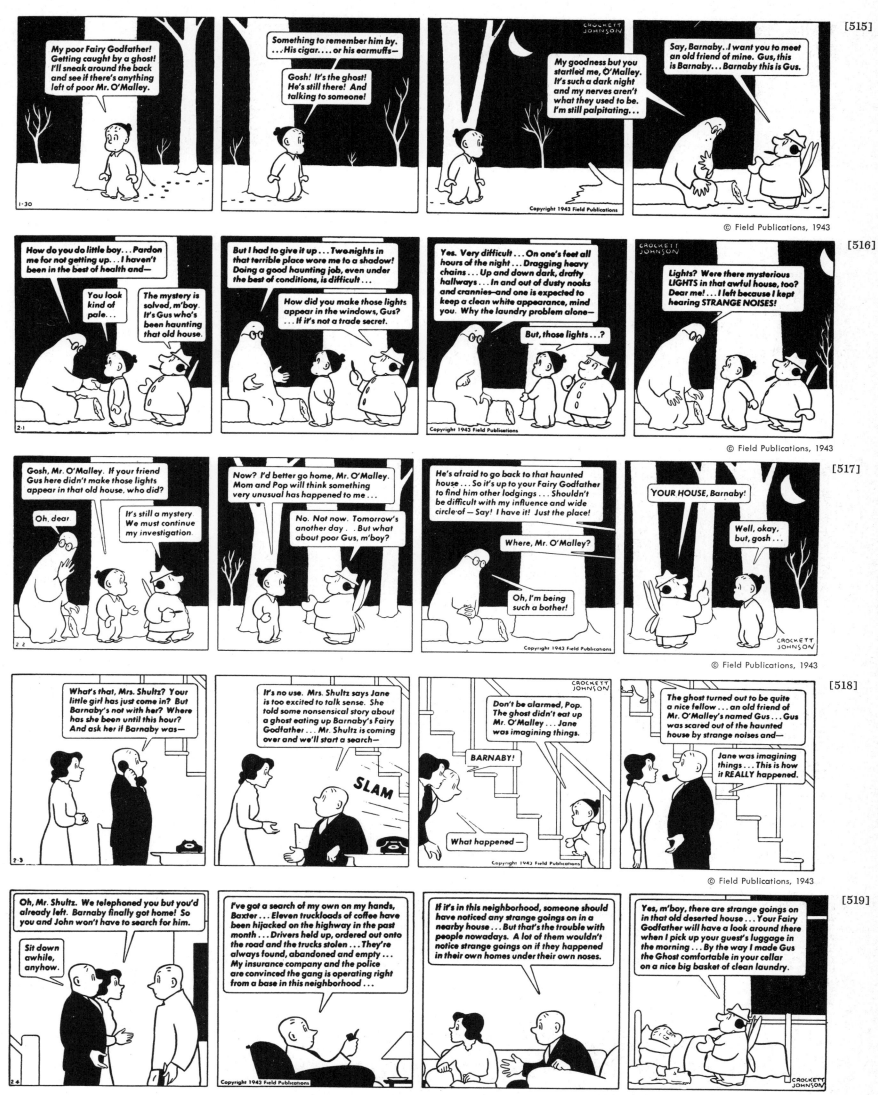

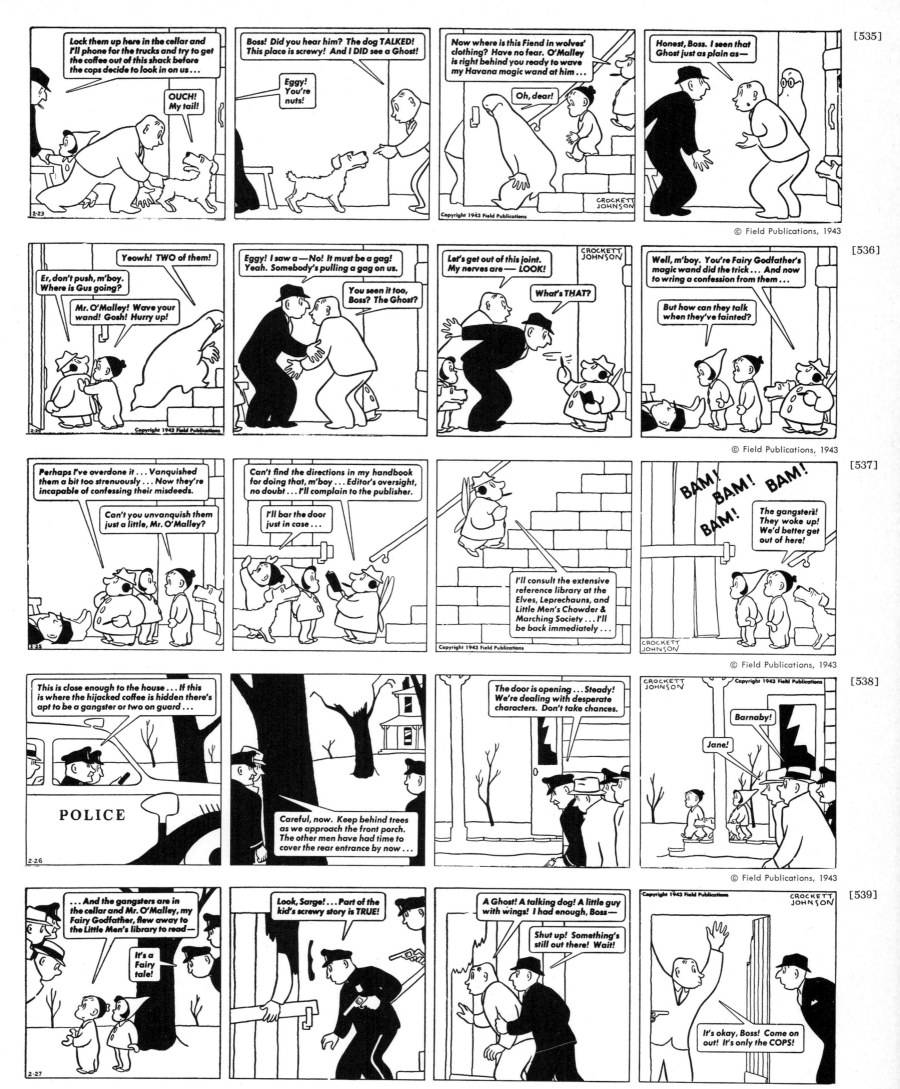

THE BUNGLE FAMILY   HIGH WORDS   By H. J. TUTHILL

[542]

© Walt Disney Enterprises, 1935

[543]

© Walt Disney Enterprises, 1935

[544]

© Walt Disney Enterprises, 1935

[545]

© Walt Disney Enterprises, 1935

[546]

© Walt Disney Enterprises, 1935

[547]

© Walt Disney Enterprises, 1935

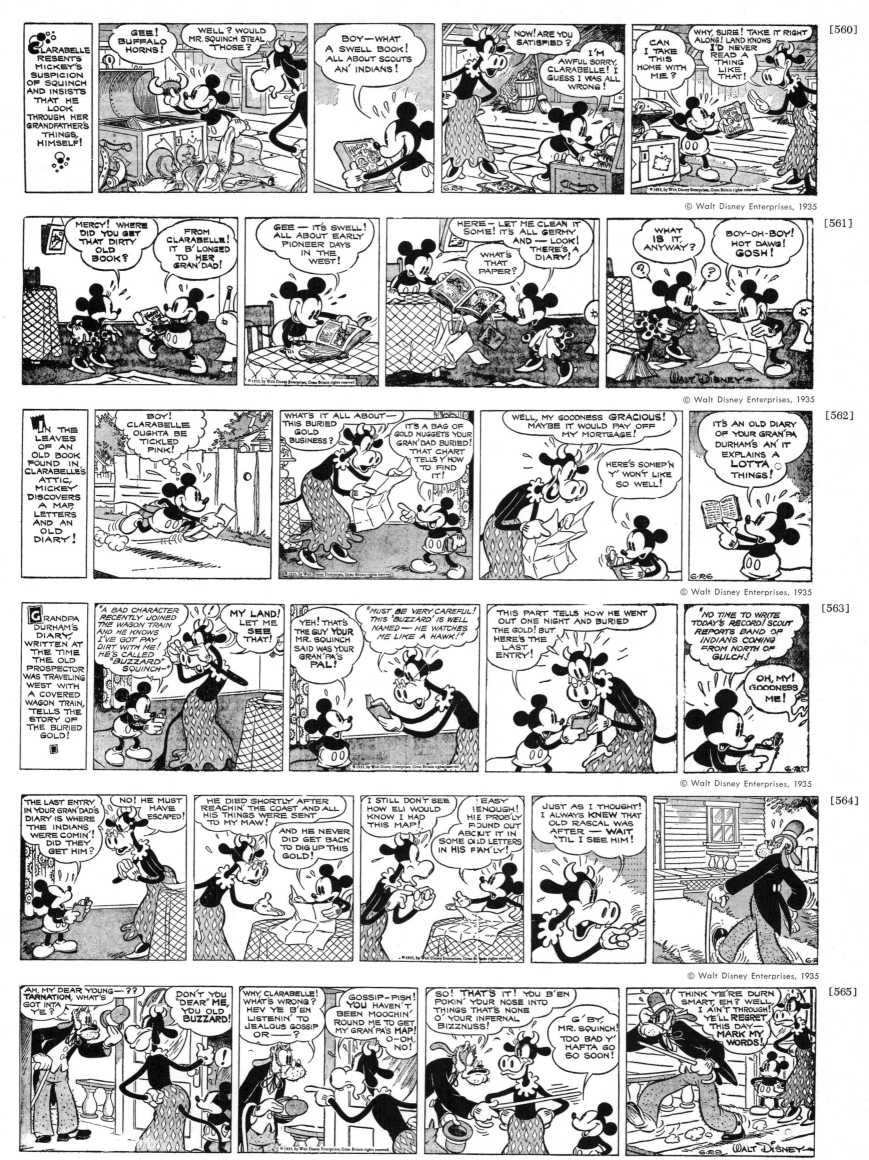

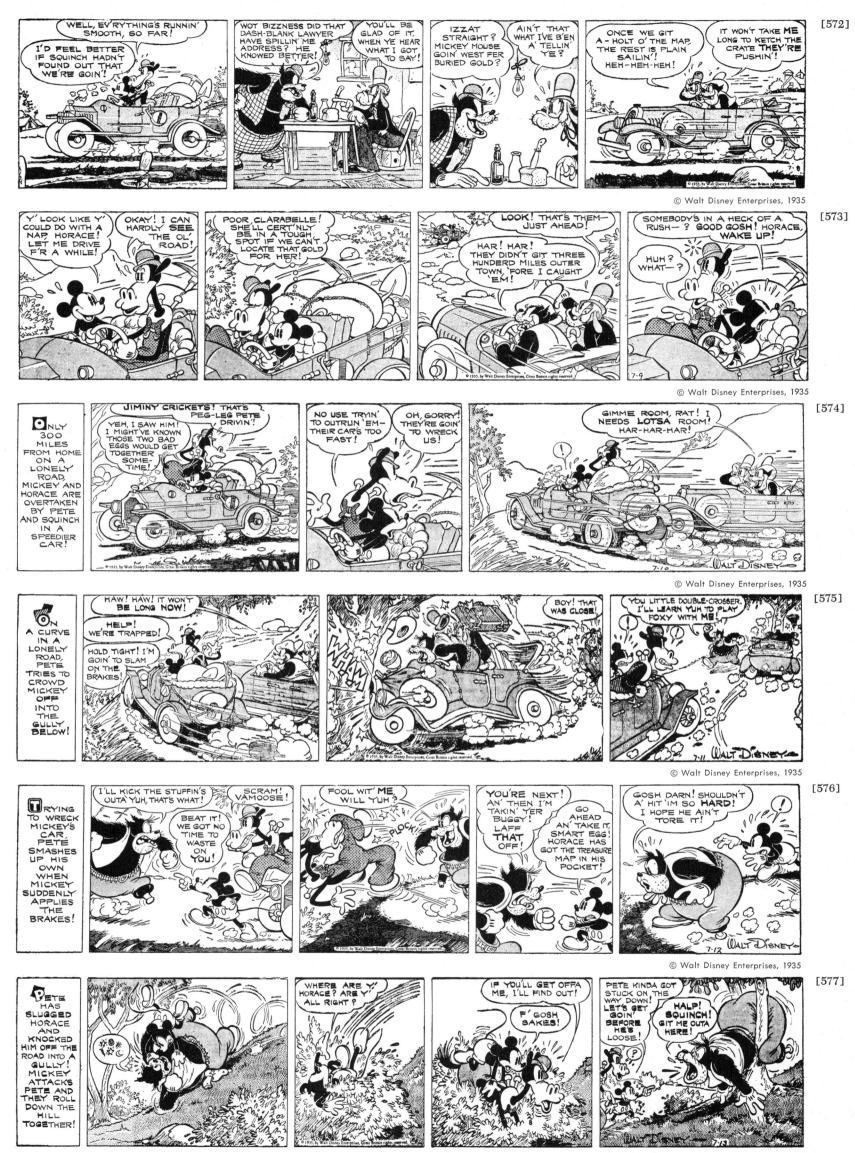

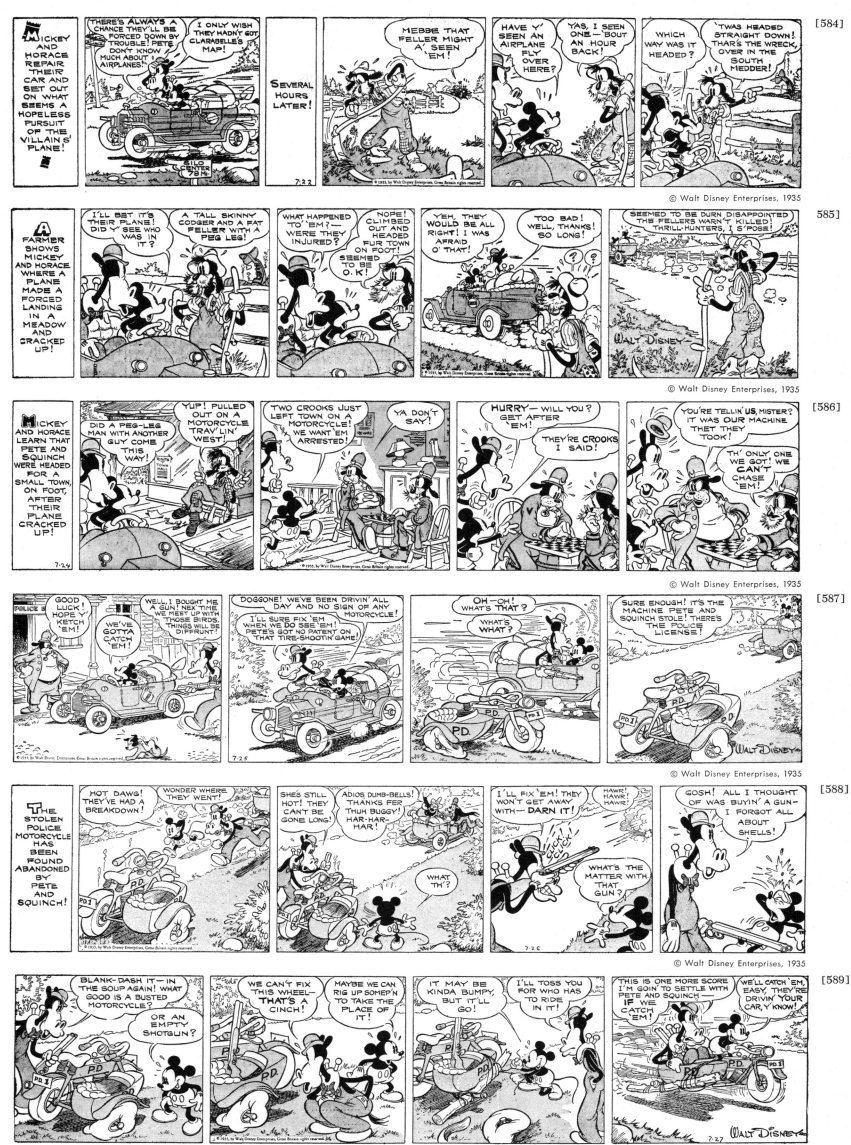

[596]

[597]

[598]

[599]

[600]

[601]

© Walt Disney Enterprises, 1935

© Walt Disney Enterprises, 1935

© Walt Disney Enterprises, 1935

© Walt Disney Enterprises, 1935

© Walt Disney Enterprises, 1935

© Walt Disney Enterprises, 1935

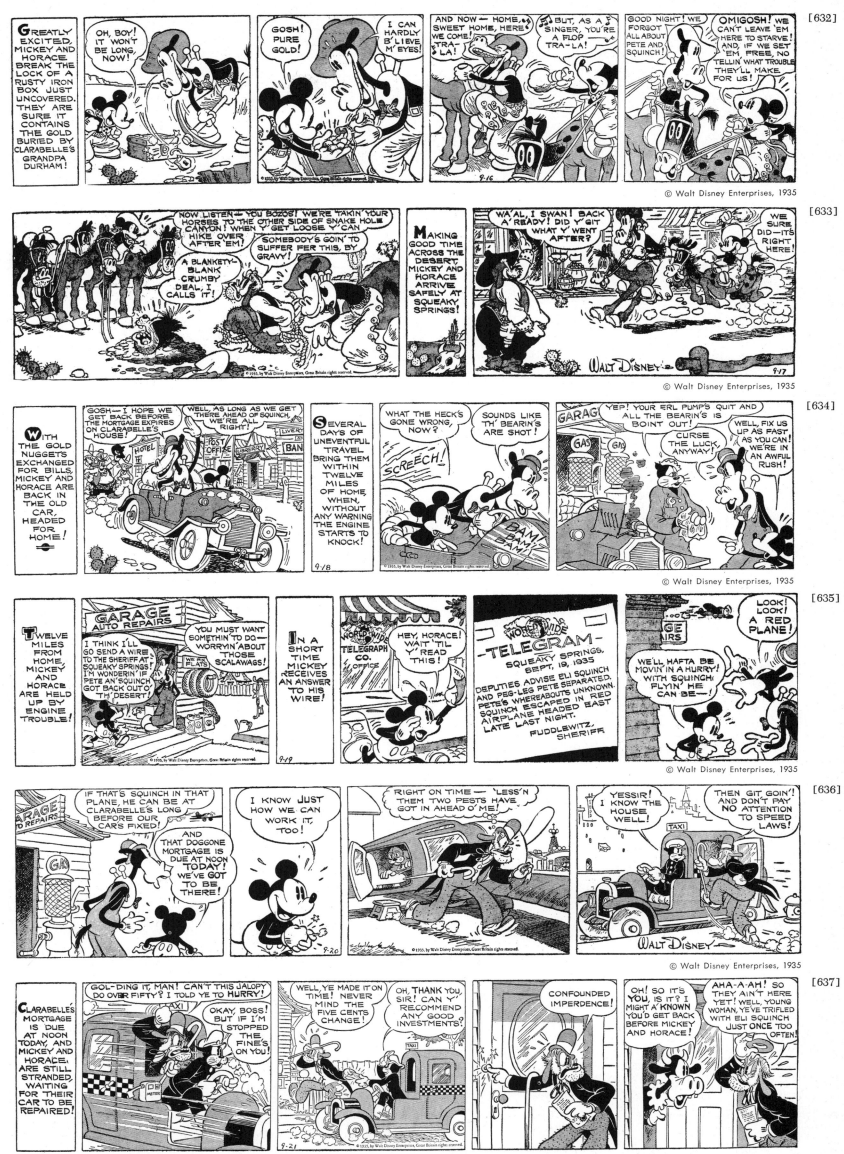

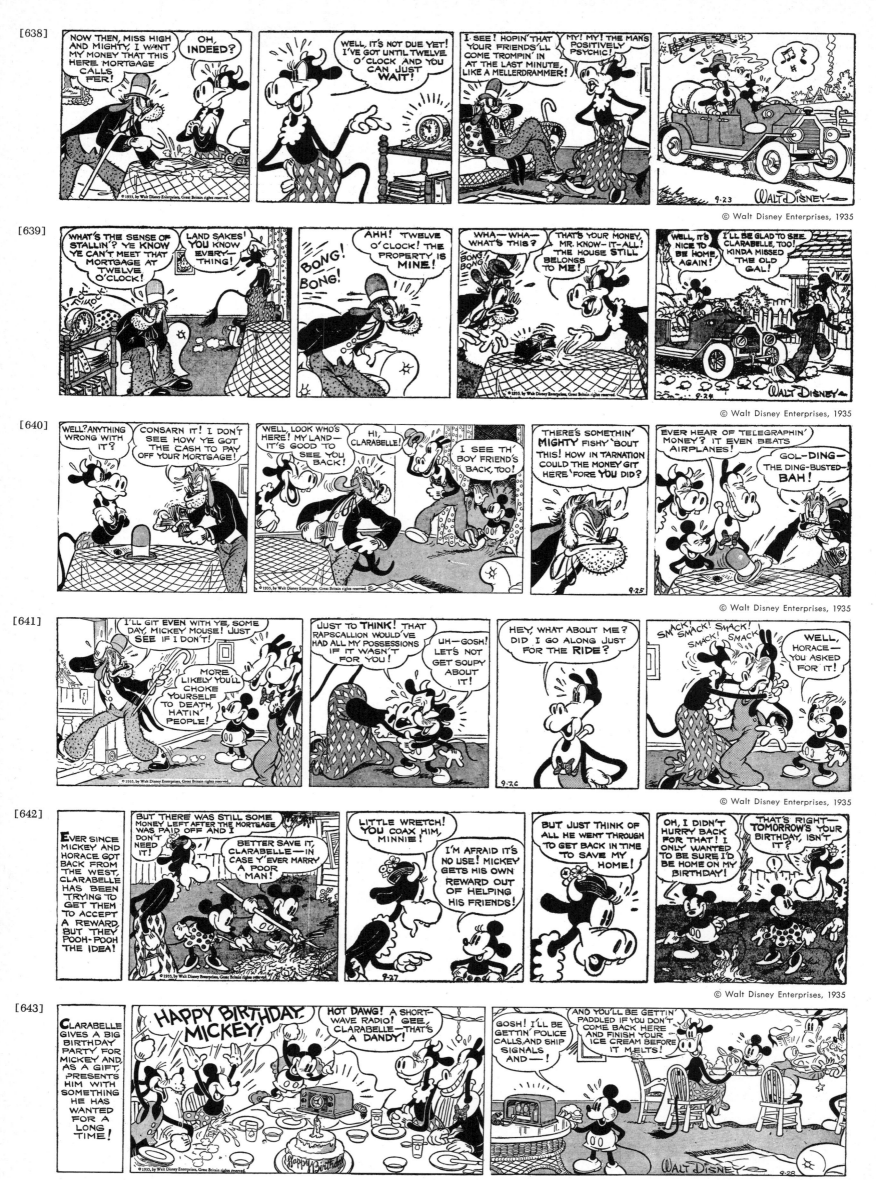

Maw Green

273

In their early days [the comic strips had an important function] as a form of crude but vigorous satire at a time when American literature in general was saccharine and imitative. The meaner and littler aspects of American life and character were lampooned in the funnies long before Sinclair Lewis discovered Main Street or Babbitt. And strip pictures caricatured U.S. manners and mores at a time when the motion picture had Mary Pickford, America's sweetheart, as its fairest flower. Corrupted by neither a literary training nor a literary tradition, taking their material from the life they observed around them, the comic-strip artists presented a series of extremely pointed (and fundamentally ill-natured) comments on the American public, which promptly roared with laughter and came eagerly back for more.

"The Funny Papers," Fortune, April 1933

© Chicago Tribune-New York News Syndicate, Inc., 1935

[710]

© Chicago Tribune-New York News Syndicate, Inc., 1935

[711]

© Chicago Tribune-New York News Syndicate, Inc., 1935

[712]

© Chicago Tribune-New York News Syndicate, Inc., 1935

[713]

© Chicago Tribune-New York News Syndicate, Inc., 1935

[714]

© Chicago Tribune-New York News Syndicate, Inc., 1935

[715]

© Chicago Tribune-New York News Syndicate, Inc., 1935

VII

Cats, Dogs, Possums, Counts, and Others

A Comics Miscellany,

1928-1950

This section offers a selection of Sunday pages from some memorable strips. The preponderance of half-page and tabloid-page layouts rather cheerlessly indicates the encroaching reduction of space allowed comic-strip artists toward the close of the strip's first half century. But the ample and colorful use of this halved area by cartoonists is sometimes admirable.

Notes on strips in this section

The first three selections in this section are all by one of the great original and inimitably individual talents in the strip field, Milt Gross, whose *Nize Baby, Count Screwloose,* and *Dave's Delicatessen* are among the most consistently and irrepressibly daffy of strips. Flowing from one into the other, with some of the same characters traipsing into one feature and out of the other, Gross's strips use names only as tags of convenience. They are all slices of the great Gross comic cheesecake from which two dozen delectable books and films were pared in his lifetime [716-718].

The comic strip *Felix the Cat* was drawn by Otto Mesmer, although it was signed by Pat Sullivan until the latter's death. Felix, a feisty, inventive, restless, yet somehow delicate adventurer in his glass menagerie world, never attained the wide strip following that the charming enchantment of his weekly and daily activities might have earned him [719].

Al Capp's irreverent and crudely hilarious *Li'l Abner,* the veritable *yawp* of the newspaper comic strip, was at a creative peak from 1934 to 1944; the examples here are from three of those *Abner* years [720-722].

Hejji was begun when the Hearst chain raised its Sunday comic section from sixteen to thirty-two pages in 1935, and it provides this wonderful example of what happened when Dr. Seuss's gorgeous lunacy moved briefly into comics [723].

Abie the Agent, Harry Hershfield's nervy and pioneering development of the first definitively Jewish strip hero, from 1914 through the thirties, was a subtle, adult work of humor and unspoken compassion, which deserves more analysis and discussion than it has received. Here are two examples in the relaxed mood which the strip acquired in Hershfield's later years [724-725].

This final selection of Herriman's Sunday *Krazy Kat* pages [726-733] are from the great color tabloid period of 1934-44, eight examples of the rare work which, during the artist's last decade, appeared consistently in only two United States newspapers, the Saturday *New York Journal* and the Saturday *Chicago American*. Herriman's comic work, a national treasure comparable to Daumier's in France, deserves the permanence of a definitive and complete collection in boards, and the dignity of republication in the original size and color from beginning to end. (Meanwhile, Nostalgia Press has provided an anthology, now available in softcover.)

Walt Kelly's insouciant *Pogo* [734-737] was a brilliant newspaper adaption, in daily and Sunday format, of a major strip which was originated and essentially perfected in comic-book format—the only instance of a comic-book creation moving wholly and permanently into the newspaper strip medium. *Pogo* became the first comic strip to have its daily episodes reprinted virtually complete in book form, sequentially, year after year.

Gus Arriola's *Gordo*, with a cast of human and animal characters, remains a daily delight in today's papers, with Sunday pages of exceptionally individual graphic design [738-739].

Casey Ruggles [741], Warren Tufts's somber, adult Western adventure strip, lasted from May 1949 until late 1954 (and was ghosted in its later months). Its strong narrative and brutal point-of-view clearly anticipated the Italian Westerns of Sergio Leone (*A Fistful of Dollars*, among others) and their imitations on both sides of the Atlantic.

Krazy Kat, the daily comic strip of George Herriman, is, to me, the most amusing and fantastic and satisfactory work of art produced in America today. With those who hold that a comic strip cannot be a work of art I shall not traffic. . . . Such is the work which America can pride itself on having produced, and can hastily set about to appreciate. . . . It is wise with pitying irony; it has delicacy, sensitiveness, and an unearthly beauty. The strange, unnerving, distorted trees, the language inhuman, unanimal, the events so logical, so wild, are all magic carpets and faery foam -- all charged with unreality. Through them meanders Krazy, the most tender and the most foolish of creatures, a gentle monster of our new mythology.

Gilbert Seldes
"The Krazy Kat That Walks By Himself," The Seven Lively Arts, 1924

Dave's Delicatessen

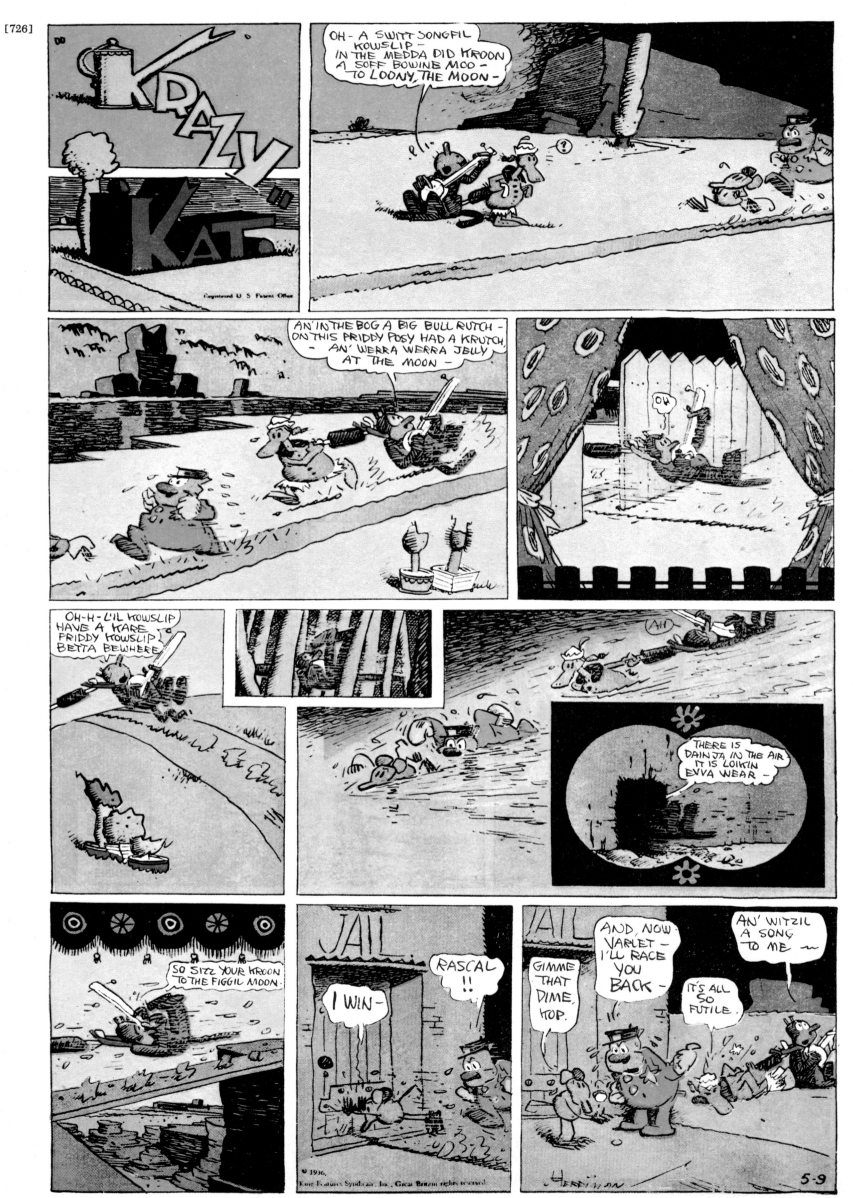

[738]

[739]

Most of the Sunday strips of the first generation of the comics were [partially] collected and republished in book form. Some . . . were brought out by standard publishers; the respected Frederick A. Stokes Company carried I know not how many 'Foxy Grandpa' and 'Buster Brown' titles for many years. Now all these books are very difficult to find; I can only conclude . . . they were literally read to pieces. I am myself the proud possessor of the Buster Brown book . . . and of a much more cherished fragment of a 'Foxy Grandpa,' but I have not encountered anything new for many years. Only the other day, a very intelligent bookseller of my acquaintance, a contemporary of my own, told me that he had never heard of these books, and not long after he proved it by offering me something utterly unrelated to them with an inquiry as to whether that was what I was talking about. It is sad to think of any man wasting his life as that man must have wasted his.

Edward Wagenknecht
As Far As Yesterday, 1968

VIII

Little People,
Wise Guys,
and Witches

The Return of the Funnies

What follows is a frankly subjective, perhaps even cursory, selection of comics, picked to represent the dominant event on the comic pages during the recent past. And much of the recent history of the comics centers on the arrival, success, and influence of Charles Schulz's *Peanuts*.

The old family strip formula has been turned completely around, for what we have is not a bunch of adults behaving like children but a group of children behaving like neurotic adults. And the traditional American "bound to win" has quite often become born to loose.

More than that, the influence of the tiny, sparse panels of Schulz's strip, plus the increasing cost of paper and printing, have shrunk the size of all comics. So that we not only see graphics clearly derivative of Schulz's style, but a general shrinkage in comics in width and depth. Indeed, the venerable *Dick Tracy* is but one example of a strip drawn so that its bottom quarter can be cropped off entirely, leaving it Schulz-size. And some papers have been known to shrink all comics back to a mere two-column width.

Suffering the most, perhaps, is the Sunday color comic section, with most comics now available in either a third-page or a quarter-page format, with panels either shrunk or cropped off or dropped out.

Comics have long had a flexible format. In the 1930s King Features cartoonists were instructed to provide three expendable panels. A full page of *Blondie*, for example, could become a half-page by dropping its companion top features, *Colonel Potterby and the Duchess*, and omitting three of its *Blondie* panels.

Currently, the different syndicates use different methods for possible squeezing, but the alert reader will notice herein several examples of the expendable (or expended) top, whereby a comic could be easily condensed by dropping its top line of panels, leaving it two deep

Another result of smaller panels is a static quality to some strips. Very good gags may be delivered, and often are, in a three-panel format which virtually repeats itself except for the dialogue balloons, an approach observable in the otherwise keenly caricatured *Tumbleweeds* sequence reproduced here.

Fewer papers using fewer strips also means fewer outlets for cartoonists, with the result that one cartoonist finds himself producing two (and sometimes more) strips in order to keep up. But more on that matter later.

For now, enough of complaints and almost enough of history. What is left is humor. Humor, and a gradual moving away from the "soap opera" strips that have dominated the comics pages for three decades. But humor of that sort has been called "adult," "sophisticated," and the rest. If it contains less out-and-out slapstick, knockabout, and tumble, however, it is still probably no more or less adult on the whole than was comics humor in the past. It is only different—and it reflects the way a United States with more citizens, more of whom have gone to college, sees itself in the 1950s, 1960s, and 1970s. In a major aspect, *Broom Hilda* is, after all, the man-chasing spinster stereotype we all know from traditional popular drama of all kinds.

Notes on strips in this section   A short-lived strip, but one much loved by devotees of comics, Jack Kent's *King Aroo* [744-749] took much the same sophisticated approach to the naif materials of the fairy tale as *Krazy Kat* had done to the animal fable or *Barnaby* had done to a child's fantasy. The choice of *King Aroo* strips here is Jack Kent's own, by the way.

The influence of *Peanuts* [742-743] on both Mell Lazarus's *Miss Peach* [756] and on Johnny Hart's *B.C.* [755] will be obvious, and is acknowledged. But Lazarus has also now given us *Momma* [759], a comics manifestation of the general consciousness of the manipulative, possessive mother, be she Jewish or gentile. And Hart is also half the team, with Brant Parker, of the quasi-medieval farce *The Wizard of Id* [757].

What has been called the "Mort Walker factory," with Dik Browne and Jerry Dumas, produces (or has produced) *Beetle Bailey, Hi and Lois, Hägar the Horrible, Boners Ark,* and *Sam's Strip.* The first three fit into dramatic-comic and strip traditions and the fourth is about those traditions. *Bailey* is "service comedy," tellingly updated [752]. *Hi and Lois* is a suburban family strip, but with a not always obvious element of distaste and even dislike [758]. Hägar, when he is not looting, is as gloriously henpecked as were Jiggs and Dagwood [753]. And *Sam's Strip* was about strips, their characters and conventions, themselves. It is therefore a fitting way to end our volume [761-763].

Meanwhile, there has been *Doonesbury* [754], which began as a student's strip at Yale, and was inspired, in its early days, probably equally by *Peanuts* and by Jules Feiffer's rhetorically conceived panel cartoons.

For our omissions in this final survey we apologize. For our brief overview of a decade and a half, we hope to incur your enlightenment and your pleasure.

Tumbleweeds   Tom K. Ryan   1971

[752]

Hägar the Horrible   Dik Browne   1974

[753]

[757]

Hi and Lois   Mort Walker   1963

[758]

Momma   Mell Lazarus   1972

[759]

[760]

Sam's Strip   Jerry Dumas   1962

[761]

[762]

[763]

A Selected, Introductory Bibliography

of Books and Articles on Newspaper Comics

Note: The editors do not recommend all of the titles listed as equally informative and factual. A number are perfunctory and sketchily researched, and the data given are often contradictory. But these *are* the best known and most readily available titles in a shallowly covered field.

Abel, Robert H., and David Manning White, eds. *The Funnies: An American Idiom.* New York: The Free Press of Glencoe, 1963.

Aldridge, Alan, and George Perry. *The Penguin Book of Comics.* Harmondsworth, England: Penguin Books, 1967.

Becker, Stephen. *Comic Art in America.* New York: Simon and Shuster, 1959.

Blackbeard, Bill. "The First (Arf, Arf!) Superhero of Them All" (on Popeye). In *All in Color For a Dime,* ed. Dick Lupoff and Don Thompson. New Rochelle, N.Y.: Arlington House, 1970.

————. "Mickey Mouse and the Phantom Artist." In *The Comic Book Book,* ed. Lupoff and Thompson. New Rochelle, N.Y.: Arlington House, 1973.

————. *Comics.* Boston: Houghton Mifflin, 1973.

———— (with Thomas Inge). "American Comic Art." In *A Nation of Nations,* ed. Peter C. Marzio. New York: Harper & Row, 1976.

————. *The Endless Art: The Literature of the Comic Strip.* New York: Oxford University Press. Forthcoming.

————, ed. Series of classic comics reprints. Westport, Conn.: Hyperion Press. Forthcoming.

Couperie, Pierre, and Maurice Horn. *A History of the Comic Strip.* New York: Crown Publishers, 1968.

Craven, Thomas. *Cartoon Cavalcade.* New York: Simon and Shuster, 1943.

Goulart, Ron. *The Adventurous Decade.* New Rochelle, N.Y.: Arlington House, 1975.

Horn, Maurice, ed. *The World Encyclopedia of Comics.* New York: Chelsea House, 1976.

Murrel, William A. *A History of American Graphic Humor.* New York: Macmillan, for Whitney Museum of American Art (2 vols.), 1933 and 1938 (o.p.)

Phelps, Donald. "Rogues Gallery/Freak Show." In *Prose* (no. 4), New York, 1972.*

Robinson, Jerry. *The Comics: An Illustrated History of Comic Strip Art.* New York: G. P. Putnam's Sons, 1974.

Sheridan, Martin. *Comics and Their Creators.* Boston: Hale, Cushman and Flint, 1942 (paperback edition: Luna Press, 1971).

Waugh, Coulton. *The Comics.* New York: Macmillan, 1947 (paperback edition: Luna Press, 1974).

* Donald Phelps, one of the most perceptive critics of the comics, is listed here for only the most readily obtainable of his magazine pieces. His other essays on the comics have been published largely in obscure, ephemeral, sometimes mimeographed little magazines like *Gnosis* or *The Mysterious Barricades.* His work on the American comic strip cries out for anthologizing.

An Annotated Index of the Comics

Abbie an' Slats began in 1937, its eccentric characters and its somewhat amorphous locale created by
[485-496]   Al Capp, who also wrote the strip for its first nine years and persuaded magazine illustrator Raeburn Van Buren to draw it. Capp was succeeded as the writer by his
brother, Elliott Caplin, who later became a prolific plotter of strips of all kinds. Caplin
continued to write *Abbie an' Slats* until the strip's demise in 1971.

Abie the Agent was first introduced by Harry Hershfield as a minor character in his burlesque melo-
[724-725]   drama *Desperate Desmond*. Abe Mendel Kabibble appeared in his own strip in 1914
as a sympathetically conceived ethnic type, a perpetually worried, fiercely active,
lower middle-class New York businessman. Hershfield himself was born in Cedar
Rapids, Iowa, and had been a journeyman cartoonist since the age of fourteen in
Chicago and San Francisco. Abie's success, and his creator's own subsequent career
as a writer and speaker and raconteur, took Hershfield to New York. Abie ceased his
life as a Hearst feature in 1940.

Alley Oop by V. T. Hamlin began his life as a Newspaper Enterprise Association feature in 1933
[432-434]   and lived it as a comic caveman. Then in 1933, Hamlin introduced Professor Wonmug
and his time-machine, and that device carried Alley forward to the twentieth century
and then backward again to any era where the possibilities for a comic adventure—
and for strong graphic design and (on Sundays) the fanciful use of color—seemed
promising. Hamlin, a native of Perry, Iowa, retired from the strip in 1971.

A. Mutt by Bud Fisher began as a sports page feature in 1907. He was joined by Jeff within
[41-46]   five months. See **Mutt and Jeff.**

A. Piker Clerk appeared in the *Chicago American* in 1904, a pioneer cross-page daily strip, with a
[47]   horse-racing background, and the direct progenitor of *A. Mutt*, above. Its author,
Clare Briggs, was born in Redsburg, Wisconsin, in 1875. Briggs was later better
known for his daily panel feature, which was variously called *When a Feller Needs a
Friend, There's One in Every Office*, and other titles, and *Mr. and Mrs.*, his Sunday
page. Briggs died in 1930.

Barnaby, Crockett Johnson's (David Leisk's) delightful, somewhat literary fantasy of a boy
[505-539]   and his cigar-chomping fairy godfather, Mister O'Malley, began in *PM* in April 1942.
The author turned the feature over to others between late 1946 and 1952, when
Barnaby was dropped, to be briefly revived in 1962. Johnson, born in 1906 in New
York, had begun as a magazine cartoonist. He turned to children's books in the 1950s
(*Harold and his Purple Crayon* and its sequels). In his later years (he died in 1975)
he devoted himself to nonobjective painting.

Barney Google and Spark Plug began as a harassed husband, an offshoot of its author Billy De Beck's previous car-
[149-150; 278-319]   toon work, but reappeared as a sports-oriented strip in the *San Francisco Herald-
Examiner* in June 1919. Barney developed into a widely popular, picaresque rogue of
the big city during the 1920s and the Great Depression era. After a wistful, knock-
kneed race horse, Spark Plug, appeared in 1922, the strip changed its name, as it
did again soon after Barney encountered the hillbilly Snuffy Smith in 1934. De Beck,
born of middle-class parents in Chicago in 1890, attended that city's Academy of
Fine Arts and went immediately into cartoon work in 1910. He died in 1942. *Barney
Google and Snuffy Smith* continues today in Fred Lasswell's version.

Baron Bean was one of George Herriman's early strips. See **Krazy Kat.**
[54-77]

B.C. first appeared as a comic strip through the New York Herald Tribune Syndicate in
[755]   1958. Its author, Johnny Hart, born in Endicott, New York, in 1931, had tried out a
similar idea of a caveman community in earlier magazine cartoons. Hart began as a

325

cartoonist in the *Pacific Stars and Stripes* when he was in the Air Force during the Korean conflict. See also **The Wizard of Id.**

Bear Creek Folks was an early strip by C. M. Payne, better known for his *S'Matter Pop?*
[24-25]

Beetle Bailey was the first (1950) of the strip successes of Mort Walker, who had already estab-
[752]   lished himself as a gag and panel cartoonist in such publications as *The Saturday Evening Post*—indeed Beetle, as "Spider," first appeared there. Walker was born in El Dorado, Kansas, in 1923 and raised in Kansas City. He received only a few casual art lessons, served in the infantry in World War II, and worked as an editor for Dell Publications in New York while cartooning in his spare time. Walker is also founder and guiding force behind the Museum of Cartoon Art in Greenwich, Connecticut. See also **Hi and Lois, Sam's Strip,** and **Hägar the Horrible.**

Blondie was begun in 1930 by cartoonist Murat "Chic" Young of Chicago as a girlie strip. It
[173]   concerned a gold digger who pursued a naive but rich playboy, Dagwood Bumstead. The strip was soon converted into the most popular matriarchal family series. Young died in 1973. The strip is continued by son Dean and John Raymond.

Bobby Thatcher, George Storm's second boys' adventure strip, set standards for graphic style, char-
[179-190]   acterizations, and narrative invention and pace between 1927 and 1937, after which Storm decided to discontinue his tale. Storm was earlier responsible for *Phil Hardy,* which began in 1925 and has been called the first boys' adventure strip.

Boob McNutt, Rube Goldberg's Sunday-only strip, lasted from 1915 to 1934. Begun as a low-comedy
[157-158]   gag strip, it was converted to comic adventure with the addition of Boob's girlfriend, Pearl, a rival named Major Gumbo, the twins Mike and Ike (they look alike), and Bertha the Siberian Cheesehound. Goldberg, born in 1883, began as a cartoonist with the campus magazine of the University of California at Berkeley, and was a major contributor to the development of the comics. Best remembered for his zany cartoon inventions, he created and drew many other comic and sports page and even editorial cartoons before he died in 1970.

Braggo the Monk was one of several alternating titles given to Gus Mager's "Monk" strips. See **Sher-**
[34]   **locko the Monk** and **Hawkshaw the Detective.**

Bringing Up Father, George McManus's low-comic saga of Jiggs, an Irish-American bricklayer made sud-
[144-145; 479-484]   denly wealthy by the Irish Sweepstakes, and Maggie, his socially ambitious wife, began as a daily strip for the Hearst papers in 1913. McManus, born in St. Louis in 1884, had been a cartoonist for that city's *Republic,* beginning at age sixteen. *Bringing Up Father* juxtaposed his broad caricatures with his fine draftsmanship and sense of space and depth. The strip has been continued beyond McManus's death in 1954 (although it had sometimes been ghosted meanwhile). See **The Newlyweds** and **Nibsy the Newsboy.**

Broom Hilda, Russ Myers's cigar-chomping, beer-guzzling witch (who claims once to have been
[760]   married to Attila the Hun), first appeared on the comics pages in 1970. Myers was born in Pittsburg, Kansas, in 1938 and spent his apprenticeship conceiving humorous greeting cards for the Hallmark Company.

Buck Nix, Sidney Smith's early humanized animal strip, began in the *Chicago Examiner* in
[92-95]   1908. See **Old Doc Yak** and **The Gumps.**

Buck Rogers concerned a twentieth-century American who awakes after a sleep of five centuries.
[427-428]   It began as pulp fiction, *Armaggedon 2415* by Phil Nowlan, and in 1929 became the first science-fiction comic strip, as plotted by Nowlan and drawn by Dick Calkins. The feature continued until 1967, the work of a number of writers and illustrators after 1947.

The Bungle Family, Harry Tuthill's penetrating burlesque of the compulsive and harassed big-city lives
[163-169; 540-541]   of George and Jo Bungle, has been called one of the most inventive and artistic of all

comic strips. It began in the *New York Evening Mail* in 1918 as *Home Sweet Home.* Tuthill, born in the Chicago slums in 1886, led the life of an itinerant salesman from the age of nine, offering everything from newspapers to fake patent medicines, while trying to teach himself a drawing style that would carry his wryly comical sense of human character and relationships. He landed his first newspaper job in St. Louis on the *Post-Dispatch* in the art department in 1910 and took some night-school art courses with the income. He folded the successful Bungles in mid-1942, apparently because of syndicate pressure to make it a more cheerful family strip, but revived it eight months later and distributed it himself. He retired in 1945 and died in St Louis in 1957.

Buster Brown was R. F. Outcault's second important strip, the adventures of a likable, upper-class [3-5]   brat, in contrast to his lower-class Yellow Kid (see **Hogan's Alley**). Outcault was born in 1863 in Lancaster, Ohio, and had established himself with gag cartoons in the old *Life* and *Judge* magazines before introducing his hearty urchins and the *Yellow Kid* to the *New York World.* Buster's adventures began in 1902 in the *New York Herald,* and, although they were discontinued in 1920, Buster and his grinning dog Tige remained familiar figures in American popular culture, even after Outcault's death in 1928.

Captain Easy was (also as *Washington Tubbs II* and *Wash Tubbs*) the premier comic adventure [435-437]   strip. It began in 1924 as a humor strip but soon began its journeys to the far corners of the real and imaginary world. Roy Crane, whose inventive and innovative graphics carried the strip as much as did his narrative fancy and sense of pace, was born in Abilene, Texas, in 1901. In 1943 Crane began *Buzz Sawyer,* while Easy and Tubbs were taken over by his former assistant, Leslie Turner. See **Wash Tubbs.**

Casey Ruggles was the work of ex-actor and radio and television scripter Warren Tufts, born in [741]   Fresno, California, in 1925. Tufts had little formal art training, but his strip work was thoroughly professional from the start. He did the short-lived science fiction strip *The Lone Spaceman,* as well as *Lance,* a full-page art feature with highly sophisticated color treatment. *Casey Ruggles* began in May 1949.

Chantecler Peck. Beyond the fact that it appeared on March 11, 1911, in Joseph Pulitzer's *New York* [38]   *World,* we can offer no further information on this feature or its artist. The popular concept of the rooster, and his name, go back to a whole series of medieval tales, of course, one of which Chaucer retold.

Count Screwloose (of Tooloose) was one of several zany strips by Milt Gross. He began it in 1929 and [717]   continued it either as the bottom or top Sunday feature until 1934, when the Count joined the company of clowns at *Dave's Delicatessen.* Gross (1895-1953) was a native of New York City who began drawing at age twelve, and created a variety of strip characters (*That's My Pop, Nize Baby*) and books of humorous doggerel verse, frequently in Yiddish dialect (*Hiawatta Witt No Odder Poems*).

Dave's Delicatessen began as a 1931 daily and Sunday feature by Milt Gross. In early 1935, it was joined [718]   by Gross's other favorite, *Count Screwloose* (see preceding).

Desperate Desmond was Harry Hershfield's first strip for the Hearst papers and a direct imitation of C. W. [37]   Kahles's *Hairbreadth Harry.* See **Abie the Agent.**

Dick Tracy was created by Chester Gould in 1931. Gould, born in Pawnee, Oklahoma, in 1900, [688-715]   the son of a newspaper publisher, had been a sports cartoonist and had done a movie-burlesque strip, *Fillum Fables.* With his plainclothes detective, he discovered an exceptional talent for strip narrative and a bizarre, sometimes brutal, sense of characterization and atmosphere.

Dok's Dippy Duck by John "Dok" Hager appeared locally in the *Seattle Times* in 1917. Hager had been [84-91]   a dental surgeon (hence the "Dok") with an interest in caricature until he moved from Terre Haute, Indiana, to Seattle in 1889 and went to work for the *Times.* He retired in 1925 because of blindness, and died in 1932 at seventy-four.

Doonesbury began as *Bull Tales* in the *Yale Record* in 1968, moved to the *Yale Daily News* the
[754] following year, and (named for one of its protagonists) moved into national newspaper syndication in late 1970. It is the work of Garry Trudeau, who was born in New
York City in 1948 and is a graduate of the Yale School of Art and Architecture. His
strip has occasionally been censored by having daily episodes dropped by subscribing papers for his satiric but candid treatment of politics, drugs, and sex.

The Family Upstairs. This was *The Dingbat Family*, George Herriman's early strip, in whose basement
[48-53] *Krazy Kat* first appeared.

Felix the Cat began as an animated cartoon, the work of Australian-born Pat Sullivan, and moved
[719] to the comics in 1923. The strip was ghosted by several hands, Otto Mesmer being
the most frequently mentioned and talented candidate.

Flash Gordon was the work of magazine and comics illustrator Alex Raymond (although he did not
[430] plot the strip), born in 1909 in New Rochelle, New York. Raymond had previously
worked with Russ Westover on *Tillie the Toiler* and Lyman Young on *Tim Tyler's
Luck*. Raymond's best work was a unique combination of physiological realism and
graphic fantasy. During the Second World War, when Raymond served in the Marine
Corps, the strip was taken over by others. When Raymond returned to civilian life,
he began the detective strip *Rip Kirby*, and continued it until he was killed in an
automobile accident in 1956.

Gasoline Alley began (at first, as a single panel) in 1918, and was devoted to the country's then-new
[151-156] fascination with automobiles. It became a family strip in which the characters aged
in "real time" (as opposed to "dramatic" or, one might say, "strip time") with the introduction of the foundling "Skeezix" on "Uncle Walt" Wallet's doorstep in 1921 and
Walt's subsequent marriage to Phyllis Blossom. The strip's author-illustrator, Frank
King, was born in Cashton, Wisconsin, in 1883 and began as a professional cartoonist on the *Minneapolis Times* in 1901. Moving to Chicago, he tried several unsuccessful strips until *Bobby Make-Believe* (in 1915) and then *Gasoline Alley*. King's gentle continuity reached its narrative best in the 1930s and 1940s. King died in 1969
but his strip has continued and is today done, daily and Sunday, by Dick Moores, who
carries on its tradition of graphic resourcefulness and interest.

Gordo, Gus Arriola's brilliant graphic fantasy on the life of a contemporary Mexican bache-
[738-739] lor, began in 1941 and featured strong characterizations and attractive graphics from
the start. Arriola, born in 1917 in Arizona, grew up in Los Angeles and worked as an
animator on MGM cartoons. He was also the only artist to suspend his daily strip
during his service in World War II and resume it after his discharge.

The Gumps, Sidney Smith's enormously popular serial drama of lower middle-class family life,
[96-102; 128-129] began in 1917, conceived by *Chicago Tribune* publisher Joseph Patterson and executed by Smith (and sometimes ghosted by others, even in its early years). Smith was
born in Bloomington, Illinois, in 1877 and had been responsible for the humanized
animal strips, *Buck Nix* and *Old Doc Yak*, in both the *Examiner* and *Tribune*. When
Smith was killed in 1935, *The Gumps* was continued by his assistant, Gus Edson.

Hägar the Horrible was begun by Dik Browne in 1973 and became an almost instant success. The title
[753] character, who looks remarkably like Browne himself, is a sort of cross between an
ancient Viking plunderer and the traditional henpecked husband and father. See **Hi
and Lois.**

Hairbreadth Harry was the work of C. W. Kahles, born in Germany in 1878 and raised in Brooklyn after
[143] the age of six. Kahles had already been a cartoonist for several years when he first
drew *Harry* in 1906. Harry began as a boy hero, but around 1916 had reached young
manhood. On Kahles's death in 1931, the strip was continued for eight more years by
F. O. Alexander.

The Hall-Room Boys was the work of illustrator-cartoonist H. A. (Harold Arthur) McGill and began in the
[35] *New York American* in 1906. It was at first a three-column, upright panel, usually di-

vided into six frames, and presented the adventures of two of Mrs. Pruyn's ambitious boarders. McGill later continued the strip as *Percy and Ferdy,* distributed by the *Sun-Herald's* syndicate. McGill died in 1952 at age seventy-six.

Hans und Fritz. See **Katzenjammer Kids.**
[7]

Happy Hooligan was the classic Irish-American tramp. Fred Opper's strip began in Hearst's Sunday
[9; 159] comic sections in both New York and San Francisco in 1900. Opper was born in Madison, Ohio, the son of Austrian immigrant parents, in 1857. Opper also introduced *Maud the Mule* and *Alphonse and Gaston,* and became a Hearst political cartoonist as well. Failing eyesight forced him to discontinue *Hooligan* and most of his other work in 1932. He died in 1938.

Hawkshaw the Detective was born out of Gus Mager's *Sherlocko the Monk* in 1913 when the American repre-
[31] sentatives of A. Conan Doyle, author of the Sherlock Holmes stories, threatened a lawsuit. Sherlocko was quickly humanized along with his assistant, now called "the Colonel." Mager discontinued Hawkshaw in mid-1922, but he was later revived as a companion feature to Rudolph Dirks's *The Captain and the Kids.* Mager sometimes did the strip on this revival, but during other periods it was ghosted (as was *The Captain*) by the gifted Bernard Dibble. Hawkshaw retired with Mager in the later 1940s. See **Braggo the Monk.**

Hejji was a Hearst-King Features Sunday page of comic fantasy by Dr. Seuss that appeared
[723] briefly in 1935. Seuss (Theodor Geisel) had previously done magazine cartoons (a well-remembered series in *Liberty*) and advertising drawings ("Quick, Henry, the Flit!" was his). He later, of course, became famous for his children's books (*The Cat in the Hat, Horton Hears a Hoo,* et al.), and he was a master of comic doggerel verse.

Hi and Lois by Mort Walker (scripts) and Dik Browne (drawing) is a suburbanite family strip
[758] which first appeared in 1954, and which frequently reverses the attitudes and characterizations of older strips in its genre. Browne was born in 1918 in New York City and worked his way up from newsboy to cartoonist on the old *New York Journal.* Before joining the Walker group, he had done advertising art. See also **Beetle Bailey** and **Hägar the Horrible.**

Hogan's Alley was one of several slum place-names given to R. F. Outcault's Sunday feature page in
[1] the *New York World.* It was also the name which stuck. *Hogan's Alley* featured a bald child in a yellow nightshirt who quickly became known as "The Yellow Kid," and Outcault's page was renamed again. See **Buster Brown.**

Jimmy, later *Little Jimmy,* was James Swinnerton's most famous strip, begun in 1904 (but
[10] appearing sporadically at first) and continuing until 1958, except for a break in the 1940s when Swinnerton switched to *Rocky Mason.* Swinnerton was born in Eureka, California, in 1875, and raised in Stockton, where his father was a newspaper publisher and politician. The younger Swinnerton began a series of weekly bear drawings, *Little Bears,* on the *San Francisco Examiner* children's page, the first continuously presented graphic character feature in a newspaper. Swinnerton also did *Mr. Jack,* the well-remembered, female-chasing, humanized tiger. He retired in 1958, turned to landscape painting, and died in Arizona in 1974.

Johnny Wise, by Thomas Aloysius "Tad" Dorgan, was a short-lived, weekly 1902 color-page effort
[2] by a man who was later and better known for his slangy sports cartoons and "Indoor Sports" panel feature. Dorgan was born to laborer parents in San Francisco in 1877 and had been urged to develop his drawing talents while recuperating from a factory accident at age thirteen. His drawing style and comic attitudes had an effect on early cartoonists and readers alike. He died unexpectedly on Long Island in 1929.

Katzenjammer Kids (in German slang of the time "the hangover kids") was begun in 1897 by Rudolph
[6; 146-148] Dirks when Rudolph Block of Hearst's *New York Journal* suggested he model a comics feature on the captioned German cartoon series of Wilhelm Busch depicting the

destructive brats *Max und Moritz.* In the result, Dirks combined strip continuity and talk balloons for the first time in comics history. Dirks was born in Germany in 1877, and emigrated to Chicago at age seven with his parents. At twenty he was selling cartoons to *Life* and *Judge,* popular humor magazines of the time. In one of the most interesting events in early comics history, Dirks went off on a European vacation in 1912 and Hearst had his feature continued. Dirks sued, and after much litigation he was awarded the rights to use his characters, but Hearst retained title to the strip. Thus Dirks began *Hans und Fritz,* later *The Captain and the Kids,* and Harold Knerr (1883-1949), of Bryn Mawr and Philadelphia, took over *Katzenjammer Kids* and continued their adventures in sometimes superbly conceived destruction. Dirks died in 1968. Both strips, however, continued into the 1970s.

The Kin-der-Kids was created by painter and illustrator Lyonel Feininger for the *Chicago Tribune* in [16-18] 1906 at the suggestion of James Keeley. Keeley undoubtedly had the Katzenjammers in mind, but Feininger wrought a motley crew of kids and adults and put them into uniquely ludicrous adventures. Feininger, born in New York in 1871, had been given a musical education in Germany by his parents. In 1894 he began a career as an illustrator for magazines there and in France and the United States. He quit the *Kids* after a few months after a contractual dispute with his publishers and pursued a successful career in painting until his death in 1956.

King Aroo is one of the most celebrated strips of the recent past in the comics, but celebrated [744-749] largely among devotees of comics, and appealing largely to members of the readership that loved *Krazy Kat, Barnaby, Pogo,* and *Little Nemo.* The King was the creation of Jack Kent, born in Burlington, Iowa, in 1920. It was probably Kent's lack of formal art training that led him to a loose-lined art style, with panels full of characters and activity. It was surely his innate artistic ability that kept those panels from looking cluttered. The strip began in 1950 in national syndication but was discontinued after a few years. It was kept on in limited syndication until 1965 by Stanleigh Arnold's small Golden Gate Features. Today Kent devotes most of his time to children's book illustration.

Krazy Kat, the most highly praised of all comic strips, was begun by George Herriman as a cat-[170-172; 726-733] and-mouse chase, a part of his *Dingbat Family* strip. Krazy got his own strip in October 1913, and thus the imaginative fantasy life of Krazy and Ignatz Mouse and the other inhabitants of Kokonino County began. It was continued, often solely because William Randolph Hearst liked it although a mass public did not, until Herriman died in Los Angeles in 1944. Herriman had been born in 1880 in New Orleans but was raised in Los Angeles. Estranged from his family, he was drawing cartoons and working as an office boy at the *Los Angeles Herald* before he was twenty. He rode the rails to New York and finally landed a staff cartoonist job at the *World* in 1901, eventually ending up with Hearst for whom he did several strips before settling down to *Krazy Kat* alone.

Li'l Abner began with almost instant success in August 1934. Cartoonist Al Capp (Alfred Cap-[720-722] lin), whether he was really aware of it or not, was offering his own feisty variation of the favorite American story of the yokel (or, in this case, Yokum) who exposes the foibles and corruptions of the city slickers simply by maintaining his own naiveté. Capp, who still manages to people his strip with memorably lampooned characters and events after more than forty years, was born in 1909 in New Haven, Connecticut, to a father who wrote and drew his own comics for the amusement of his family. Capp attended a number of art schools and did some work at the Associated Press before he became an assistant of Ham Fisher, creator of *Joe Palooka.*

Little Joe was a Sunday feature by Ed Leffingwell, Harold Gray's cousin, assistant, and letterer [438-439] on *Little Orphan Annie.* The story concerned a thirteen-year-old on a modern cattle ranch owned by his widowed mother and managed by Utah, a cowhand with a shady past. Gray himself wrote and drew much of the strip. When Ed Leffingwell died his

brother, Robert, who also assisted Gray, took over as *Joe's* nominal author. The strip continued into the late 1950s in both the *Chicago Tribune* and *New York Sunday News* comic sections.

Little Nemo
[11-14; 140-142]
undoubtedly grew out of Winsor McCay's earlier *Dreams of a Rarebit Fiend* (1904), which showed the nightmarish results of his protagonist's overeating. Nemo first appeared as *Little Nemo in Slumberland* the following year in the *New York Herald,* and represented pictorially the feelings and transformations experienced in the dreams of McCay's boy protagonist. When McCay moved to Hearst's papers in 1911, he simply retitled his feature *In The Land of Wonderful Dreams* and continued Nemo's nocturnal adventures until 1914. Nemo reappeared in 1924, this time back in the *Herald* (and, of course, its syndicate) until 1927. McCay was born in Spring Lake, Michigan, in 1869 and received basic art instruction from a teacher in Ypsilanti. When he was seventeen he was in Chicago seeking more instruction but working professionally on posters as well. He began as a cartoonist on the *Cincinnati Enquirer* in 1903. McCay was also a pioneer in film animation, beginning in 1909. His best-known movie cartoon is *Gertie the Trained Dinosaur,* but he had also earlier filmed a Nemo fantasy. Next to George Herriman's, McCay's comics work has probably received the widest recognition and praise. He died in 1934.

Little Orphan Annie
[644-672]
reputedly began as a boy in Harold Gray's original conception, and was changed to a redheaded orphan girl by Joseph Patterson of the *New York News.* In any case, her narrative began in 1924 and lasted beyond her creator's death in 1968 in continuations of ever-decreasing interest until reprints of Gray's earlier strips replaced them. Gray was born in Kankakee, Illinois, in 1894 and served his apprenticeship assisting Sidney Smith on *The Gumps.* With *Annie* he established a feature of exceptional narrative interest and pace. Although, of course, Gray did use assistants, he hired no ghosts either to draw or plot *Annie,* and maintained his personal interest in his work for forty-five years.

Mama's Angel Child,
[23]
Esther, was the work of Penny Ross of whom little is known except that he was a man, and that he had assisted Outcault on *Buster Brown* and possibly ghosted that strip on occasion.

Maud
[8]
was established as *And Her Name Was Maud* as a topper strip to Fred Opper's *Happy Hooligan* in 1926. But the character of the grinning, stubborn, kicking mule, Maud, had been used by Opper in his earlier strips. See **Happy Hooligan.**

Merely Margy
[161]
began as *Oh! Margy* in the late 1920s and was a comics effort by John Held, Jr., who was and is best known for his depiction of leggy, flat-chested 1920s "flappers." Born in 1889, Held was from Salt Lake City. He had begun as a cartoonist when barely sixteen, and had also been a sports page and, later, magazine illustrator on *Vanity Fair* and *The New Yorker. Margy* lasted until 1935. Held died in 1958, having long since turned to sculpture.

Mickey Mouse
[542-643]
was not the first star of animated cartoons to gain a strip of his own, but he had one by January 1930. Three months later, when the Walt Disney studios turned the project over to Floyd Gottfredson, and he introduced broadly burlesqued adventure and melodrama as its basis, the strip began to thrive. By the early 1950s, however, King Features, which distributed the feature, had urged the elimination of all action-adventure from humor strips, and Mickey returned to a domestic gag-a-day. Gottfredson, born in 1907 in Kaysville, Utah, was delighted with the comics as a young man, and took correspondence courses in cartooning. He moved to Hollywood, applied at Disney's, and was put on as an apprentice animator. Until 1938, he also did the frequently charming Mickey Mouse Sunday color strip.

Midsummer Day Dreams
[40]
by Winsor McCay. See **Little Nemo.**

Minute Movies,
[191-196]
the creation of Edgar Wheelan, began as Midget Movies in 1918. It not only parodied movie serials, it also helped establish the idea of continuity in the daily strip.

Wheelan created his own imaginary studio and stable of stereotypical stars and contract players (Ralph McSneer, Hazel Deare). He cast them in mysteries, adventures, love stories, and (later) the classics. The strip lasted on the comics pages until the mid-1930s (but later appeared in new episodes in the *Flash Comics* book). Wheelan was born in San Francisco in 1888, and graduated from Cornell. His mother had been a comic-strip cartoonist, and he began with the Hearst papers as an editorial and sports cartoonist. He died in Florida in 1966.

Miss Peach first appeared to instant success in 1957. Admittedly and obviously inspired in part by
[756] *Peanuts,* the feature was the work of Mell Lazarus, born in Brooklyn, New York, in 1927, where, as he has said, he hated school and "even flunked art in high school." See **Momma.**

Momma was Mell Lazarus's second successful strip, introduced in late 1970. A comic-strip ver-
[759] sion of the possessive, manipulative "Jewish mother," if the term is taken to mean a generic and descriptive and not necessarily ethnic type. See **Miss Peach.**

Moon Mullins, Frank Willard's winning rogue, put in his first appearance in the *Chicago Tribune* in
[138-139; 221-277] 1923, partly as an answer to Hearst's success with *Barney Google.* As the strip accumulated characters of its own (Kayo, Emmie Schmaltz, Lord Plushbottom, Mamie, Uncle Willie) and a narrative pace of its own, it became one of the classics of the comics page. Willard was born in the Chicago area in 1893, the son of a physician, and he early determined to become a cartoonist. He died suddenly in 1958. His assistant (and sometime ghost) Ferd Johnson continued *Moon,* but today the continuities of its past are gone and it is a gag strip.

Mr. E. Z. Mark was the work of F. M. Howarth (1870 ?-1908), whose strip drawing in *Puck* in the
[32] 1890s probably helped pave the way for the comic strip. In 1903 he was approached by William Randolph Hearst and the result was the *Lulu and Leander* pages. Howarth never employed talk balloons, even in the Hearst section.

Mr. Jack, James Swinnerton's humanized, pop-eyed, skirt-chasing tiger, first appeared as a sep-
[33] arate feature in late 1902 and ran almost weekly until early 1904. It was revived as an occasional daily from 1912 to 1919, only to be revived again as a top feature above *Little Jimmy* in the 1930s. See **Jimmy.**

Mr. Twee Deedle was a Sunday feature, a fantasy-fairy tale for small children by Johnny Gruelle, crea-
[20] tor of Raggedy Ann. The strip replaced *Little Nemo* in the *New York Herald* when Winsor McCay moved his feature over to Hearst. Gruelle, born in Illinois but raised in Indianapolis, was the son of a landscape painter, and was a cartoonist with the *Indianapolis Star* and *Cleveland Press* when still in his late teens. He contributed illustrations, cartoons, and children's stories to a number of magazines, and wrote the Raggedy books and others. Gruelle lived in Connecticut after 1910. He returned to the comics with the Sunday strip *Brutus* in the late 1930s. He died in Miami in 1938.

Mutt and Jeff began as *A. Mutt,* when H. C. "Bud" Fisher established the first continually published
[28-29; 108-125; 136-137] six-days-a-week strip on the *San Francisco Chronicle* sports page on November 15, 1907. Fisher, born in Chicago in 1885, left for a job at the *Chronicle* during his third year at the University of Chicago. His unique drawing style and comic point of view developed quickly during the early years when he did the strip himself, moving it from syndicate to syndicate as the value of his services rose. Fisher died in 1954, but the strip had by then been ghosted for years. And, of course, it continues today.

The Naps of Polly Sleepyhead was Peter Newell's contribution to the early comics page. Newell, better known for
[21] his fanciful children's books (*Topsys and Turvys, The Hole Book, The Slant Book*), was born in Bashnell, Illinois, in 1862 and was largely self-taught, although he did some work at the Art Students League in New York. He died in 1927.

Naughty Pete was the work of Charles Forbell, who was best known for his cityscape and architec-
[22] tural perspective drawings in *Puck, Life,* and *Judge.* It appeared in *Judge* from after

1910 until its demise in the late 1930s. The "& A.C." appended to Forbell's name (and that of other cartoonists) was for Arthur Crawford, a cartoonist's agent and gagman.

The Newlyweds (or *The Newlyweds and Their Baby*) was the feature which George McManus did
[19] for Pulitzer's *World* between 1904 and 1912. When he moved over to Hearst in that latter year, McManus renamed the feature *Their Only Child*. When his *Bringing Up Father* had established itself by 1918, he discontinued *Their Only Child*. But in the 1930s, he brought it back on Sundays as *Snookums*, a cofeature to *Maggie and Jiggs*. See **Bringing Up Father.**

Nibsy the Newsboy, another early George McManus feature, appeared in the *New York World* between
[15] April 1905 and late July 1906. Nibsy's imagination could turn any New York street into "Funny Fairyland" and a kind of lower-class takeoff on *Little Nemo*. See **Bringing Up Father.**

Nize Baby, by Milt Gross (his first Sunday color page), appeared in the *New York World* (and
[716] its syndicate) between 1927 and 1929. However, the wild adventures of the nefarious infant and Looy Dot Dope were abandoned by the restlessly inventive Gross for *Count Screwloose.*

Old Doc Yak was Sidney Smith's very successful transformation of his *Buck Nix* when he moved
[103-107] from the *Chicago Examiner* to the *Chicago Tribune*. See **The Gumps** and **Buck Nix.**

Our Boarding House, with the braggart Major Hoople, began in 1923 as a single daily panel in comics form
[497-504] for Newspaper Enterprise Association. On his Sunday page, the Major (in true strip form) was joined by the top-of-the-page "Nut Brothers" (Ches and Wall) in a surreal comic fantasy. The strips were the creation of Gene Ahern, born on Chicago's South Side in 1895. He attended the Chicago Art Institute for three years, hoping simply to acquire enough technique to become a funny cartoonist. Ahern moved to King Features in 1936, doing a variant of the same *Boarding House* strip as *Room and Board*, while his former syndicate continued *Our Boarding House,* and does still. Ahern died in 1960.

Out Our Way began national distribution in November 1921 as a single-panel, daily feature and
[175-178] soon developed a set of memorable recurring characters and a unique comic viewpoint. The author was J. R. Williams, born in Nova Scotia in 1888 of American parents, and raised in Detroit. He left home to shift for himself in his mid-teens, worked the railroads, and did a hitch in the cavalry before settling into a factory job, where he did his first cartooning for the company's catalog. After Williams's death in 1957 his drawings were frequently reissued by his syndicate, NEA, while his former assistant, Ned Cochran, contributed new ones to the series.

Peanuts, introduced on October 2, 1950, by Charles Schulz, revived interest in the humor strip,
[742-743] recast the size and shape of strips and the format of the comics page, and became one of the great success stories of the comics. Schulz was born in Minneapolis in 1922 and studied art by a correspondence course before he graduated from high school. He had placed a few gag panel cartoons in newspapers and the *Saturday Evening Post* before finally placing his strip, which he originally wanted to call *L'il Folks,* with United Features Syndicate.

Pogo, by ex-Disney animator Walt Kelly, actually began as a feature in *Animal Comics* in
[734-737] 1943 under the title *Bumbazine and Albert the Alligator*. In it, Pogo the Possum was initially a minor character at best. Very soon the clownish Albert was more prominently featured, Bumbazine (a boy) dropped out, and Pogo got a bigger role. By the time that Kelly moved the feature to newspaper format in the short-lived *New York Star* in 1948, it had become simply *Pogo,* and in it humanized animals daily dramatized the idiosyncrasies of their human counterparts. The political spoofs for which the strip probably became best known in the mid-1950s had actually been implicit somewhat earlier. (See nos. 734-737.) Kelly was born in Philadelphia in 1913, the son of a painter of theatrical scenery. He had been a reporter and cartoonist for the

Bridgeport Post just out of high school. When Kelly died in 1973, *Pogo* was briefly continued by others but was soon withdrawn by Kelly's widow, who devotes herself to editing books which collect his work.

Polly and Her Pals (at first *Positive Polly* in 1912) was begun as one of several "daughter" strips of the
[130-135] period. Its author was Cliff Sterrett, born in Fergus Falls, Minnesota, in 1883. He attended the Chase Arts School in New York for two years, and he began as a staff artist for the *New York Herald* in 1904, moving to the *Times* in 1908. However, Sterrett wanted to be a cartoonist, and three years later he began four different strips for the New York *Evening Telegram*. Settling on *Polly*, he gradually developed one of the most whimsically individual graphic styles in the comics section, particularly on his Sunday color work. He and *Polly* retired in 1958 and he died December 28, 1964.

Popeye. See **Thimble Theatre.**

Prince Valiant began in 1937 as a carefully researched, meticulously illustrated Sunday saga of imag-
[431] inary Arthurian times. It was created by Harold R. "Hal" Foster, born in Nova Scotia in 1892. In 1921 the ambitious young Foster bicycled his way to Chicago, to the Art Institute, National Academy of Design, and Chicago Academy of Fine Arts. He was an established advertising illustrator when the syndicators of a new *Tarzan* text-and-illustration strip approached him. Foster did the first daily *Tarzan* sequence in early 1929 and later did the Sunday episodes from 1931 until he began *Prince Valiant*. He retired from the drawing of *Prince Valiant* in 1971 but continued to plot his tale. See **Tarzan.**

Sam's Strip, unsuccessful with the public, was a well-remembered effort to make a comic strip
[761-763] which fondly spoofed the conventions, characters, and history of comic strips. Mort Walker conceived the idea with Jerry Dumas, who did the art. Dumas, born in Detroit in 1930, had very little formal training, but has been cartooning steadily since his school days. He assists on most of the Walker strips, lettering, penciling, inking. See **Beetle Bailey** and **Hi and Lois.**

School Days was one of several Sunday and daily strips by Clare Victor Dwiggins (1874-1959)
[26-27; 197-208] which depicted the almost idyllic small town life of a group of school boys. One of his strips was an authorized version of Mark Twain's *Tom Sawyer and Huck Finn*. Dwiggins was himself born in rural Ohio and attended country schools. He undertook cartooning while working as an architectural draftsman. He drew *School Days* from 1917 to 1932. Between 1945 and his death, Dwiggins worked as a book illustrator.

Secret Agent X-9 was begun by Hearst's King Features Syndicate in 1932 as one of several efforts to
[475-478] answer the success of the *Chicago Tribune-New York Daily News* detective feature, *Dick Tracy*. The syndicate hired mystery writer Dashiell Hammett to plot (he did the first four sequences) and Alex Raymond to illustrate. The strip has been through numerous transmutations since that time, with various writers and illustrators contributing. It continues today as *Secret Agent Corrigan*. See **Flash Gordon.**

Sherlocko the Monk was Gus Mager's Holmes burlesque, later transformed into *Hawkshaw the Detec-*
[36] *tive*. See the latter and also **Braggo the Monk.**

Skippy began his cartoon life in the pages of the old humor magazine *Life* as a somewhat sar-
[174] donic ten-year-old commentator on the passing scene and the world adults had made. In 1928, *Skippy* became a King Features comic strip, daily and Sunday, and continued until Percy Crosby withdrew the feature in 1943, in protest against its unauthorized commercial use. Crosby, whose drawing style was always closer to sketch-illustration than cartoon, was born in Brooklyn, New York, in 1891 and did newspaper and strip work on the *New York World* and for the McClure Syndicate before *Skippy* attracted the attention of King Features. He died in 1964.

Slim Jim, an early and all-but-forgotten strip, was drawn variously by several cartoonists, most
[30] notably by its originator, Charles Frink (who died in 1912), and his successor, Ray-

mond Ewer, who contributed our fine selection here. *Slim Jim* began as *Circus Solly* in 1910, and continued until 1937, mostly distributed to rural papers.

S'Matter Pop? was one of several similar titles assigned to the best-known strip of Charles M. Payne.
[39; 160] Payne was born in Queenstown, Pennsylvania, in 1873. He hung around the offices of the *Pittsburgh Post* and offered cartoon ideas while still a teenager; later, he was hired by the paper as a staff cartoonist. *S'Matter Pop?*, notable for Payne's decorative use of the page as well as its humor, began in the *New York World* in 1919 and continued for thirty years. Payne died in poverty and obscurity in New York in 1964, the victim of a mugging. See **Bear Creek Folks.**

The Smythes was a Sunday feature in the *New York Herald Tribune* (and its syndicate) by *New*
[126-127] *Yorker* illustrator and art editor Rea Irvin (1881-1972). Irvin was from San Francisco and was an established magazine illustrator and cartoonist both before and after his stylized interlude on the comics page.

Somebody's Stenog, distributed by the *Philadelphia Public Ledger's* syndicate, was one of the best of sev-
[162] eral "working girl" strips that began in the late 1910s. It was the work of A. H. Hayward, who was hired away from the *New York Herald* by the *Ledger.* The strip lasted into the late 1940s.

Stumble Inn was another of George Herriman's early strips. See **Krazy Kat.**
[78-83]

Tarzan, Edgar Rice Burroughs's jungle lord—a titled English heir raised from infancy by a
[429] tribe of African great apes—entered the comics page via a daily illustration-and-text strip rendered by Hal Foster in early 1928. Foster also did the Sunday version between 1931 and 1937, including the much celebrated "Lost Egyptians" sequence. See **Prince Valiant.**

Terry and the Pirates began in late 1934, the work of Milton Caniff who revitalized the style of newspaper
[673-687] adventure strips with his effective use of impressionist graphic techniques and his somewhat exotic adventure narrative. Caniff was born in Hillsboro, Ohio, in 1907. He had done several features, most notably *Dickie Dare*, before approaching Captain Joseph Patterson of the *New York News* with *Terry.* The strip was his answer to Patterson's expressed desire for a "blood and thunder" suspense adventure strip "with a juvenile angle." *Terry* was taken over by George Wunder when Caniff began *Steve Canyon* in early 1947.

Texas Slim and Dirty Dalton, a Sunday-only slapstick cowboy strip, was the work of Ferd Johnson, who otherwise
[740] assisted Frank Willard on *Moon Mullins* (and continued that latter strip after Willard's death). Johnson was born in 1905 in Spring Creek, Pennsylvania, and was drawing published cartoons before he entered high school. He attended the Chicago Academy of Fine Arts in 1923, but his first job resulted from his spending most of his time hanging around the cartoonist's desk at the *Tribune,* where he attracted Willard's sympathetic attention. *Texas Slim* began in 1925.

Thimble Theatre, by E. C. Segar, is one of the most celebrated comic-adventure strips. It began as Wil-
[443-474] liam Randolph Hearst's idea of one way to replace his recently lost *Minute Movies.* It was the work of Elzie Crisler Segar, born in Chester, Illinois, in 1894, the son of a house painter. He diligently taught himself to draw, with the help of a correspondence school course, and presented himself at the *Chicago Herald,* where he got his first work. Once founded, *Thimble Theatre* developed a set of running characters, chiefly the spinsterish Olive Oyl and her hustling brother, Castor. Popeye the Sailor first appeared in an adventure in January 1929, and immediately captivated the strip's growing audience, as well as its author. A series of memorable adventures and characters (J. Wellington Wimpy, the Sea Hag, Alice the Goon, the Jeep) followed. Segar generally kept the story continuity in his daily episodes separate and used his Sunday pages for self-contained gags. On the one occasion when he broke with that practice, he produced the masterly "Plunder Island" adventure which is

reproduced here. Segar died in late 1938. His feature has been continued since by others, but usually with quite different intention and quality.

Toonerville Folks, Fontaine Fox, Jr.'s daily panel and Sunday strip on the engaging eccentrics who in-
[209-220; 442] habited his imaginary, then still semirural suburbs, was begun in early 1915. The vignettes of the trolley's Skipper, the tough kid Mickey "Himself" McGuire, the terrible-tempered Mr. Bang, and the rest, lasted until 1955. Fox, born in 1884 in Louisville, Kentucky, went to work for the *Louisville Courier* right out of high school, doing reporting and cartoon work. He later briefly attended the University of Indiana, but dropped out to become a full-time cartoonist. *Toonerville Folks* began in the *Chicago Post* before the Wheeler Syndicate distributed it nationally. Fox died in 1964.

Tumbleweeds is the work of Tom K. Ryan, born in Anderson, Indiana, in 1926, who always wanted
[750-751] to be a cartoonist. He began in commercial art, read Western novels, and eventually did a burlesque Western comic strip. *Tumbleweeds* began modestly in 1965 and has built gradually in popularity since.

Wash Tubbs, by Roy Crane, began as *Washington Tubbs II* in 1924. See **Captain Easy.**
[320-426]

White Boy first appeared as a Sunday, half-page strip in the *Chicago Tribune* in 1933 and sub-
[440-441] sequently also in the *New York Daily News*. The strip, initially concerning a white youngster captured by an Indian tribe in the late nineteenth century, went through several changes of focus, format, and even historical time. In them, fantasy narrative switched to realism, switched to gags, and back again, possibly in efforts to appeal to juvenile readers. The feature was the work of Garrett Price, best known for his illustrations for magazine fiction and his *New Yorker* cartoons. *White Boy* became *Skull Valley* toward the end and disappeared in August 1936. Price, born in Bucyrus, Kansas, graduated from the University of Wyoming and the Art Institute of Chicago, and continued art studies in France.

The Wizard of Id is the collaborative effort of Brant Parker (ideas and drawing) and Johnny Hart
[757] (ideas). Parker, a Californian born in Los Angeles in 1920, was a Disney cartoonist and later an illustrator for International Business Machines. He judged an art show in Endicott, New York, that included the work of a highschooler named Johnny Hart in the late 1940s and a friendship developed. The vaguely medieval *Wizard* first appeared in 1964.